The Wyckoff Methodology in Depth

HOW TO TRADE FINANCIAL MARKETS LOGICALLY

Rubén Villahermosa Chaves

All rights reserved. No part of this work may be reproduced, incorporated into a computer system or transmitted in any form or by any means (electronic, mechanical, photocopying, recording or otherwise) without the prior written permission of the copyright holders. Infringement of these rights may constitute a crime against intellectual property.

Rubén Villahermosa, 2019
Independently published
ISBN: 9781703876123

Index of contents

Richard Wyckoff 15

Part 1 - How Markets Move 17
Chapter 1 - Waves 19
Chapter 2 - The price cycle 21
Chapter 3 - Trends 25
   Types of trends 26
Chapter 4 - Assessing trends 29
  Strength/weakness analysis 29
    Speed 30
    Projection 30
    Depth 31
  Lines 32
    Horizontal lines 33
    Trend lines 34
    Channels 36
    Inverted lines 38
    Converging lines 39
Chapter 5 – Trading Ranges 41

Part 2 - The Wyckoff Method 45
Chapter 6 - Wyckoff Methodology Structures 47
  Basic scheme of accumulation #1 48
  Basic scheme of distribution #1 52
  Basic scheme of distribution #2 54

Part 3 - The Three Fundamental Laws 55
Chapter 7 - The law of supply and demand 57
  Theory 57
  Price shift 59
    Initiative 59
    Lack of interest 61

Chapter 8 - The Law of Cause and Effect 63
Elements to bear in mind 64
Point and Figure Graphics 65
Technical analysis for projection of objectives 67

Chapter 9 - The Law of Effort and Result 69
The importance of volume 69
Harmony and divergence 69
   In the development of a candle 71
   On the next scroll 72
   In the development of the movements 73
   By Waves 74
   By reaching key levels 75
Effort/Result in Trends 76
Lack of interest 76

Part 4 - The processes of accumulation and distribution 79

Chapter 10 - Accumulation 81
Stock control 82
The law of cause and effect 82
Handling maneuvers 83
Counterparty, liquidity 84
The path of least resistance 84
Common characteristics of the accumulation ranges 85
Beginning of the bullish movement 85

Chapter 11 - Reaccumulation 87
Stock Absorption 88
Duration of the structure 88
Reaccumulation or Distribution 88

Chapter 12 - Distribution 89
The law of cause and effect 90
Handling maneuvers 90
Counterparty, liquidity 91
The path of least resistance 92

    Common characteristics of the distribution ranges 92
    Beginning of the Bearish Movement 93
Chapter 13 - Redistribution 95
    Redistribution or accumulation 96
    Stock control 96
    Duration of the structure 96

Part 5 - Events 99
Chapter 14 - Event #1: Preliminary Stop 101
    How the preliminary stop appears on the graphic 102
    The psychology behind the preliminary stop 103
    Uses of the preliminary stop 104
    Preliminary Support 104
    Preliminary Supply 106
Chapter 15 - Event #2: Climax 109
    Keys to climax 110
    How the climax appears on the graph 110
    The psychology behind the climax 111
    Uses of Climax 112
    Selling Climax 113
    The Selling Climax of exhaustion 114
    Buying Climax 116
    The Buying Climax of exhaustion 118
Chapter 16 - Event #3: Reaction 121
    The implications of its development 121
    The anatomy of the reaction 122
    Reaction Uses 123
    Automatic Rally 124
    Why the Automatic Rally takes place 125
    Automatic Reaction 126
    Why Automatic Reaction Occurs 127
Chapter 17 - Event #4: Test 129
    Secondary Test 129

    Functions of the Secondary Test 130
    Secondary Test Features 131
    The Secondary Tests of Phase B 132
    Secondary Test on the upper end 133
    Secondary Test on the lower end 134
The generic test 136
Where to look for tests 137
    Test after shock 137
    Test after breakout 137
    Trend test 138
How the Test appears on the graph 138
The difference between the Secondary Test and the Generic Test 140

Chapter 18 - Event #5: Shaking 141
    Addition game 0 141
    Behavior 142
    How the Spring appears on the graph 143
    Shaking functions 144
    Indications to know if we are facing a potential shakeout . 146
    Avoid labeling errors 146
Spring/Shakeout 147
    Types of Spring 148
    The Ordinary Shakeout 152
    The Spring test 152
UpThrust After Distribution (UTAD) 153
    The minor Upthrust After Distribution 154
    The Upthrust After Distribution Test 155
    Terminal Upthrust 156
    Ordinary Upthrust 156

Chapter 19 - Event #6: Breakout 157
    Change of Character 158
    How it appears on the graph 158
    Keys to the breakout event 160

Breakout does not offer an opportunity 162
Sign of Strength.. 163
　Minor SOS 164
　Sign of Strength Bar.. 164
Sign of Weakness 165
　minor SOW 166
　Sign of Weakness Bar.. 166

Chapter 20 - Event 7: Confirmation................................ 169
　How the confirmation appears on the graph 170
　Warning signal after breakout 172
　Operational Opportunity... 173
　Quantify the entry trigger 174
Last Point of Support... 176
Last Point of Supply 177

Part 6 - Phases.. 179
Chapter 21 - Phase A: Stopping the previous trend............ 181
Chapter 22 - Phase B: Building the Cause 183
Chapter 23 - Phase C: Test 185
Chapter 24 - Phase D: Trend within range...................... 187
Chapter 25 - Phase E: Trend out of range 191

Part 7 - Trading.. 193
　1. The context.. 195
　2. The structures 196
　3. Operational areas... 198
Chapter 26 - Primary positions....................................... 201
In Phase C 201
　Entry into the shake.. 202
　Entry into the shake test 203
　Entry into the Last Point of Support............................ 203
In Phase D.. 203
　Entry into the trend movement within the range 204

Entry into the break test (Confirmation Event No. 7).... 206
In Phase E 206
Summary table of trading opportunities........................ 209

Chapter 27 - Decision-making.. 211
The concept of the significant bar 211
The concept of reversal of movement................................ 213
Position Management... 215
Calculate the size of the position 216
Entry 217
Stop Loss 219
Take Profit 223

Part 8 - Case Studies 229
S&P500 Index ($ES) 231
Pound/Dollar cross ($6B) 233
Euro/Dollar cross ($6E) 235
Bitcoin (BTCUSDT).. 237
Inditex (ITX) 239
Google (GOOGL)... 241
Australian Dollar/US Dollar cross ($6A) 243
Thank you for buying this book! 245
Bibliography.. 251

Richard Wyckoff

Richard Wyckoff (1873-1934) became a Wall Street celebrity.

He was a forerunner in the investment world as he started as a stockbroker at the age of 15 and by the age of 25 he already owned his own brokerage firm.

The method he developed of technical analysis and speculation arose from his observation and communication skills.

Working as a Broker, Wyckoff saw the game of the big operators and began to observe through the tape and the graphics the manipulations they carried out and with which they obtained high profits.

He stated that it was possible to judge the future course of the market by its own actions since the price action reflects the plans and purposes of those who dominated it.

Wyckoff carried out its investment methods achieving a high return. As time passed his altruism grew until he redirected his attention and passion to education.

He wrote several books as well as the publication of a popular magazine of the time *Magazine of Wall Street*.

He felt compelled to compile the ideas he had gathered during his 40 years of Wall Street experience and bring them to the attention of the public. I wanted to offer a set of principles and procedures about what it takes to win on Wall Street.

These rules were embodied in the 1931 course *The Richard D. Wyckoff Method of Trading and Investing Stocks. A course of Instruction in Stock Market Science and Technique* becoming the well-known Wyckoff method.

Part 1 - How Markets Move

Chapter 1 - Waves

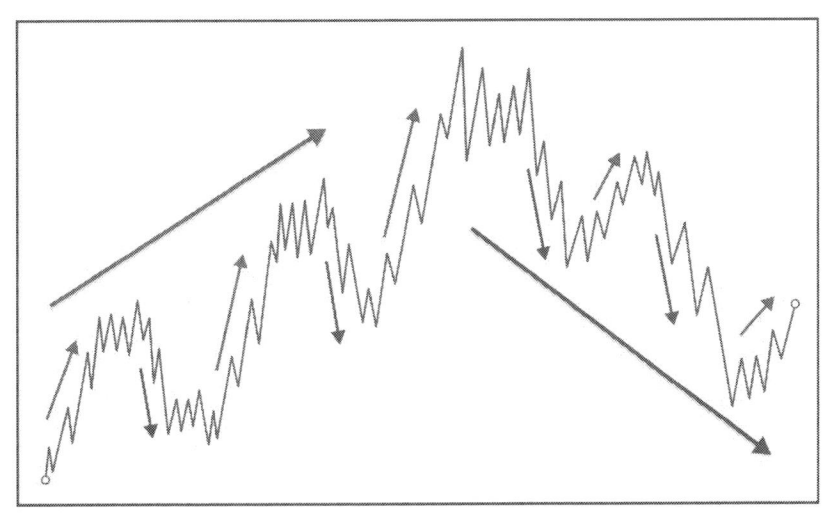

Movements by waves

Wyckoff and the first readers of the tape understood that the movements of the price do not develop in periods of time of equal duration, but that they do it in waves of different sizes, for this reason they studied the relation between the upward and downward waves.

The price does not move between two points in a straight line; it does so in a wave pattern. At first glance they seem to be random movements, but this is not the case at all. The price is shifted up and down by fluctuations.

Waves have a fractal nature and interrelate with each other; lower grade waves are part of intermediate grade waves, and these in turn are part of higher grade waves.

Each uptrend and downtrend is made up of numerous minor uptrend and downtrend waves. When one wave ends, another wave starts in the opposite direction. By studying and comparing the relationship between waves; their duration, velocity and range, we will be able to determine the nature of the trend.

Wave analysis provides a clear picture of the relative changes between supply and demand and helps us judge the relative strength or weakness of buyers and sellers as price movement progresses.

Through judicious wave analysis, the ability to determine the end of waves in one direction and the beginning in the opposite direction will gradually develop.

Chapter 2 - The price cycle

In the basic structure of the market there are only two types of training:
- Trends. These can be bullish if they go up, or bearish if they go down.
- Trading ranges. They can be of accumulation if they are at the beginning of the cycle, or of distribution if they are in the high part of the cycle.

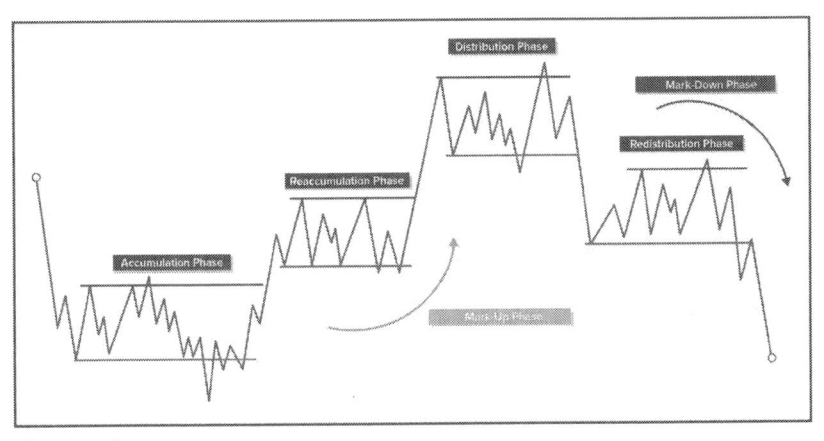

The price cycle

As we have already seen, the displacement of the price during these Phases is done by means of waves.

During the accumulation phase, professional operators buy all the stock that is available for sale on the market. When they are assured by various manoeuvres that there is no longer any floating bid, they begin the upward trend phase. This trend Phase is about the path of least resistance. Professionals have already verified that they will not encounter too much resistance (supply) that would prevent the price from reaching higher levels. This concept is very important because until they prove that the road is free (absence of sellers), they will not initiate the upward movement; they will carry out test maneuvers again and again. In case the offer is overwhelming, the path of least resistance will be down and the price at that point can only fall.

During the uptrend, buyers' demand is more aggressive than sellers' supply. At this stage, there is the participation of large operators who are less well informed and the public whose demand shifts the price upwards. The movement will continue until buyers and sellers consider the price to have reached an interesting level; buyers will see it as valuable to close their positions; and sellers will see it as valuable to start taking short positions.

The market has entered the distribution phase. A market ceiling will be formed and it is said that the big operators are finishing distributing (selling) the stock they previously bought. There is the entry of the last greedy buyers as well as the entry for sale of well-informed operators.

When they find that the path of least resistance is now down, they begin the downtrend phase. If they see that demand is present and with no intention of giving up, this resistance to lower prices will only leave a viable path: upward. If you continue to climb after a pause, this structure will be identified as a reaccumulation phase. The same is true for the bearish case: if the price comes in a bearish trend and there is a pause before continuing the fall, that lateral movement will be identified as a redistribution phase.

During the downtrend sellers' supply is more aggressive than buyers' demand so only lower prices can be expected.

Being able to determine at what stage of the price cycle the market is at is a significant advantage. Knowing the general context helps us avoid entering the wrong side of the market. This means that if the market is in a bullish phase after accumulation we will avoid trading short and if it is in a bearish phase after distribution we will avoid trading long. You may not know how to take advantage of the trend movement; but with this premise in mind, you will surely avoid having a loss by not attempting to trade against the trend.

When the price is in phases of accumulation or uptrend it is said to be in a buying position, and when it is in Phases of distribution or downtrend it is said to be in a selling position. When there is no interest, that no campaign has been carried out, it is said to be in neutral position.

A cycle is complete when all stages of the cycle are observed: accumulation, uptrend, distribution, and downtrend. These complete cycles occur in all temporalities. Therefore, it is important to consider all the time frames; because each of them can be at different stages. It is necessary to contextualize the market from this point of view in order to carry out a correct analysis of it.

Once you learn to correctly identify the four price phases and assume a totally impartial viewpoint, away from news, rumors, opinions and your own prejudices, taking advantage of your operative will be relatively easier.

Chapter 3 - Trends

Prices change and the waves resulting from those price changes generate trends. The price is moved by a series of waves in the direction of the trend (impulses), which are separated by a series of waves in the opposite direction (reversals).

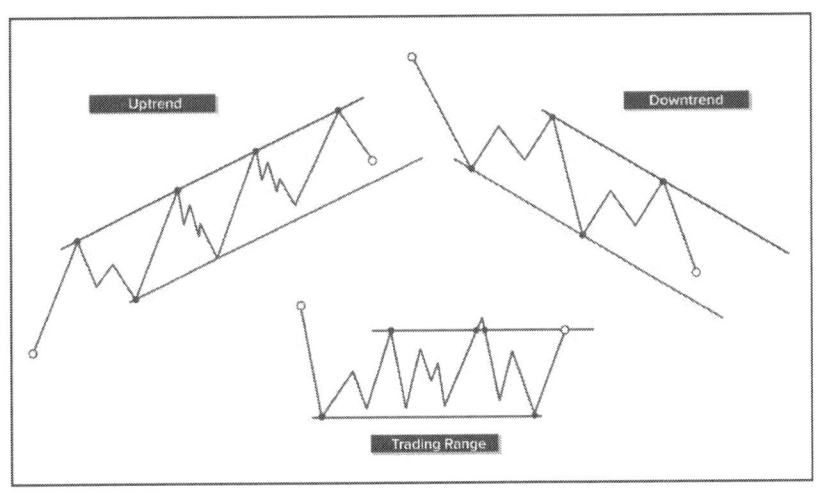

Types of trends

The trend is simply the line of least resistance as the price moves from one point to another because it follows the path of least resistance; therefore, the trader's job is to identify the trend and trade in harmony with it.

When a market is rising and encounters resistance (sales), either exceeds that resistance or the price will turn; the same happens when the price is falling and encounters resistance; either exceeds those purchases or the price will turn. These pivot points are critical moments and provide excellent locations to operate.

Depending on the direction of movement, we can differentiate three types of trends: bullish, bearish and lateral. The most objective description of an uptrend is when the price makes a series of rising impulses and falls, where highs and lows are increasing all the time. Similarly, we identify a bearish trend when highs and lows are decreasing, leaving a series of decreasing impulses and regressions. Finally, we determine a sideways environment when highs and lows remain fluctuating within a price range.

Trends are divided by their duration into three different categories; long, medium and short term. Since there are no strict rules for classifying them according to the timeframe, they can be categorized according to how they fit into the top. That is, the short-term trend will be observed within the medium-term trend, which in turn will be within the long-term trend.

Types of trends

Note that all three trends may not move in the same direction. This can present potential problems for the operator. In order to be effective, doubts must be eliminated as much as possible and the way to do this is to identify in advance the type of trading to be carried out.

A very important condition to consider when selecting the type of trading is the timing (entry calibration). Success in any kind of operative mainly requires a good Timing; but success in short term trading requires a perfect Timing. Because of this, a beginner should start with long-term trading until he achieves consistent success.

Because trends may be different depending on the time frame, it is possible but difficult to have buy and sell positions at the same time. If the medium-term trend is bullish, you can take a buy position with the expectation of holding it for a few weeks or months; and if in the meantime a short term bearish trend appears, you can take a short sell position and hold the buy trade at the same time.

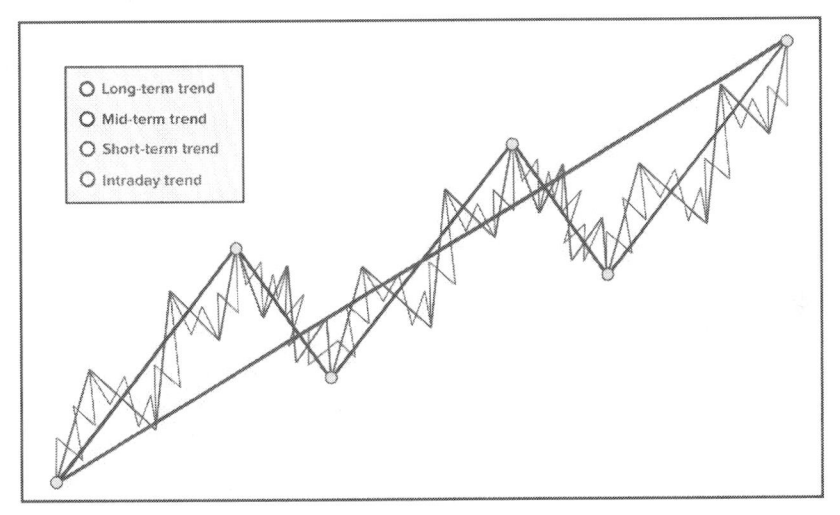

Temporalities

Although theoretically possible, it is extremely difficult to maintain the discipline necessary to maintain both positions at the same time. Only experienced operators should do this. For the initiate it is best to operate in harmony with the trend and not to operate on both sides simultaneously until consistently profitable.

You must learn and understand the motives, behavior patterns, and emotions that control the market. A bull market is driven by greed, while a bear market is driven by fear. These are the main emotions that drive the markets. Greed leads to paying higher prices until it leads to what is known as an overbought condition. On the other hand, the panic caused by falls leads to wanting to get rid of positions and sell, adding more momentum to the collapse until over-selling conditions are reached.

Having these emotions is not a negative thing, as long as they know how to move towards a positive aspect and it is very clear that what is really important is the protection of capital.

Chapter 4 - Assessing trends

This interaction between supply and demand as a trend develops will leave clues in the conformation of the price action. We have different tools to help us assess trends.

Judiciously assessing the trend is key to determining your health. It allows us to detect if any force gives symptoms of weakness or if the opposing force is gaining strength. Our job is to go for strength and against weakness.

Strength/weakness analysis
When the price is in trend, we expect greater strength from the pushing side. We have to see it as a battle between buyers and sellers where we will try to analyze the strength or weakness of both. The best way to assess current strength/weakness is to compare it with previously developed movements.

A weakness in the price does not imply a change of trend, it is simply a sign of loss of strength and tells us that we must be prepared for future movements.

There are several ways to analyze market strength/weakness. The key is comparison. Absolute values are not sought. It is a question of comparing the current movements with the previous ones.

Speed

Speed refers to the angle at which the price moves; so if the price is moving faster than in the past, there is strength. If on the other hand it is moving slower than in the past, it suggests weakness.

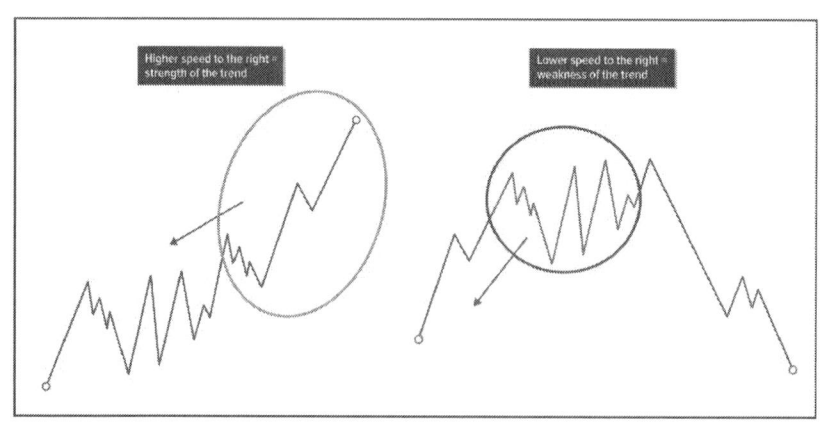

Speed Analysis

Projection

With this tool we evaluate the distance that the impulses travel and compare them with the previous ones to determine if the strength has increased or decreased.

For a trend to remain alive, each impulse must surpass the previous impulse. If an impulse is not able to make new progress in the direction of the trend, it is an alert that the movement may be nearing its end.

Distance of the impulse:

- The distance between 3 and 4 is greater than the distance between 1 and 2 = trend strength.
- The distance between 5 and 6 is less than the distance between 3 and 4 = trend weakness.

Distance between extremes:

- The distance between 2 and 3 is greater than the distance between 1 and 2 = trend strength.

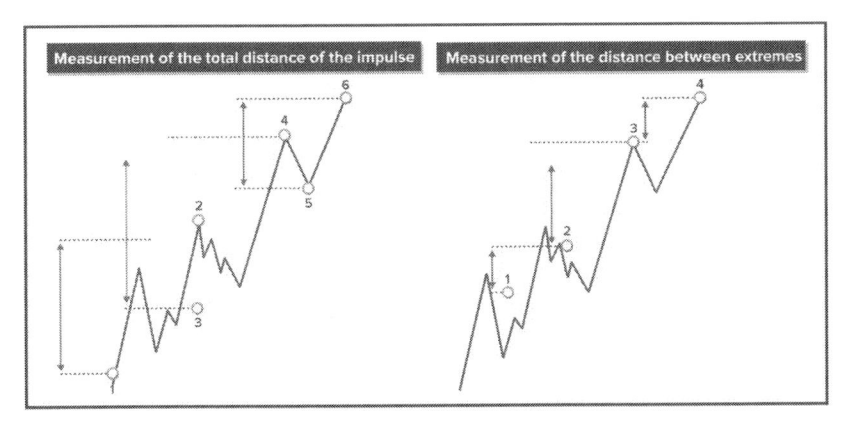

Projection Analysis

The distance between 3 and 4 is less than the distance between 2 and 3 = trend weakness.

Depth
With depth analysis we evaluate the distance travelled by trend reversals to determine whether weakness has increased or decreased.

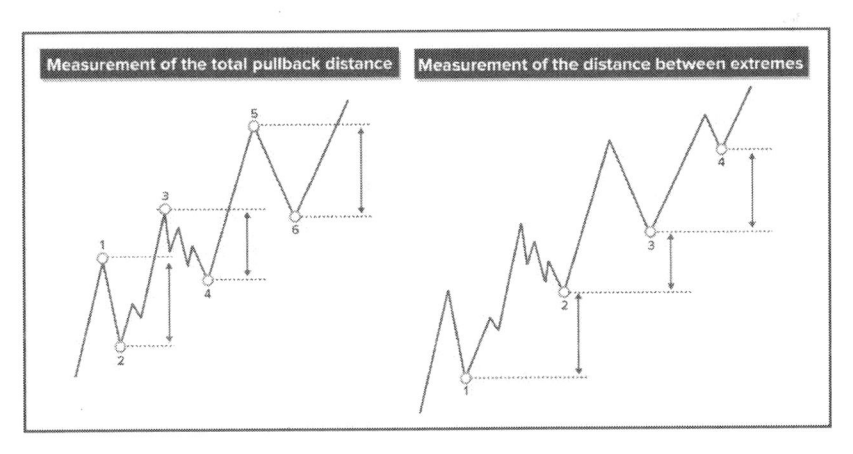

Depth Analysis

As with projection analysis, we can evaluate depth using two measurements: the total distance of the recoil from its origin to its end; and the distance the price travels from the previous end to the new end.

Pullback distance:
- The distance between 3 and 4 is less than the distance between 1 and 2 = trend strength.
- The distance between 5 and 6 is greater than the distance between 3 and 4 = trend weakness.

Distance between extremes:
- The distance between 2 and 3 is less than the distance between 1 and 2 = trend weakness.
- The distance between 3 and 4 is greater than the distance between 2 and 3 = trend strength.

Lines

The lines delimit the ranges and define the angle of advance of a trend. They are of great visual aid for the analyses, being very useful to evaluate the health of the movement; so much to identify when the price reaches a condition of exhaustion, as to value a possible turn in the market.

In general they help us to foresee levels of support and resistance at which to wait for the price. At the same time, an approach or touch of those lines suggests the search for additional signs to look for a turn, offering diverse operative opportunities.

The more touches a line has, the more validity the level for the analysis will have. You must be careful not to draw lines indiscriminately, especially on every minor movement. The correct handling of lines requires good judgment; otherwise it will cause confusion in your reasoning.

When the price penetrates a line we must remain more alert and be prepared to act. Depending on the position where the break occurs, as well as the action itself, we can suggest different scenarios. A thorough understanding of price and volume action is needed to determine the most likely scenarios.

Horizontal lines

A horizontal line identifies an old zone of imbalance between supply and demand. When it connects at least two price minima it identifies a support. This is an area where buyers appeared in the past to outdo sellers and stop the price drop. On that area it is expected that buyers will appear again when it is visited again.

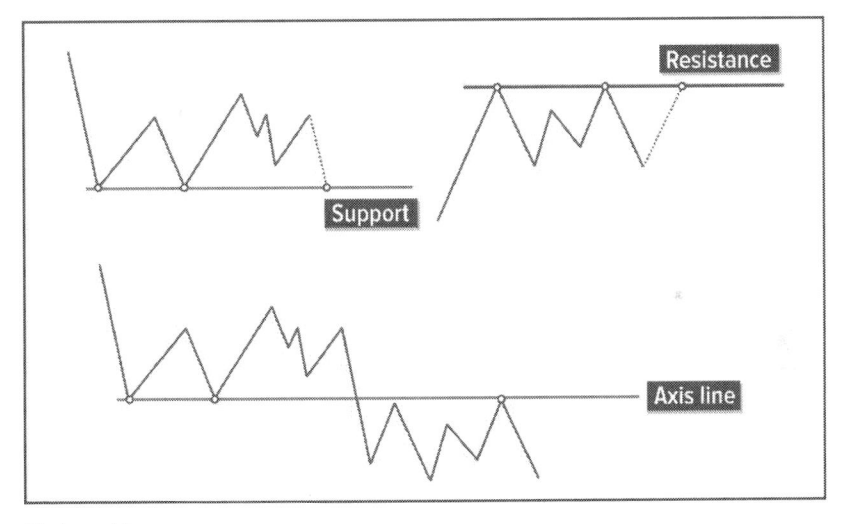

Horizontal lines

A horizontal line connecting at least two highs identifies a resistance and is an area where supply outpaced demand by stopping a price hike; that is why sellers are expected to reappear on a new visit in the future.

When a line serves both as support and resistance, it is known as a shaft line. Prices tend to revolve around those axis lines. Those price levels are constantly changing roles; a broken resistor becomes a support, and a broken support becomes a resistor.

Trend lines

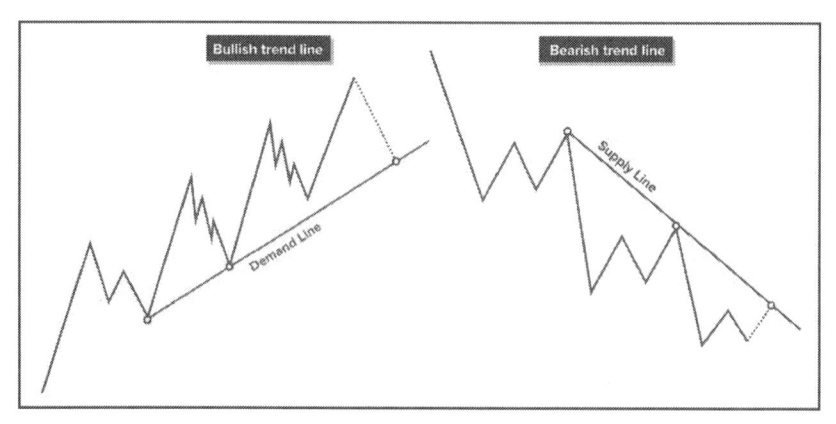

Trend lines

After identifying the nature of the trend, the next step is to build a guideline in order to take advantage of the movement. It is the simple connection between two or more price points.

In a bearish trend, the trend line is drawn by connecting two decreasing highs. This line is called the bid line because it is assumed that the sellers will appear on it.

In an uptrend, the trendline is drawn by connecting two rising lows. This line is called a demand line because it marks the point where buyers are supposed to appear.

We can continuously readjust the trend lines in order to adjust the one that best suits the price action and therefore generated the most touches. The more times the line has been respected, the stronger we will be able to interpret it when it is played again in the future.

Note that a line with too much slope will be broken too soon, so it will not be drawn correctly.

As long as the price remains within the established levels, it is said that the movement is healthy and it is appropriate to consider maintaining or adding positions.

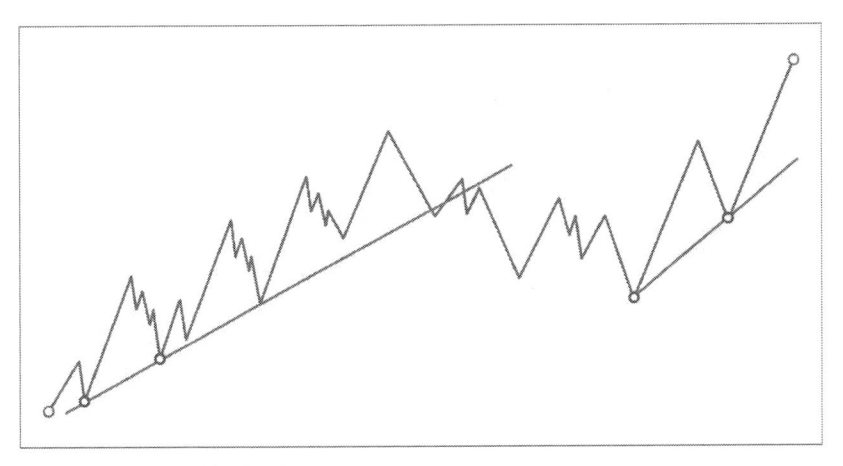

Example of false trend line breakage

When the price approaches a trend line there is a threat of breakout and this may mean that the strength of the trend is being exhausted, suggesting a change in the speed of the trend or a definite danger of reversal of the trend.

Breakout a trend line by itself is not a conclusive symptom of anything, as it may be a true or false break. What is significant is how the line is broken, the conditions under which it happens, and the behavior that precedes it.

After a movement of a certain distance, the price may find resistance to continue and this will cause the trend to change its speed and rest. During the break (lateral movement or range) the force that originally drove the trend may be renewed or even strengthened, resulting in a continuation of the trend with greater momentum than before.

Under these conditions, it is necessary to reposition the trend lines to conform to the new set angle. For this reason it should not be accepted that the mere fact of breakout the trend line is a reversal of the same.

Channels

The ideal channel will have several touch points and should capture most of the price within its limits.

When the bullish trend line or demand line is dragged towards the opposite end and anchored parallel to the maximum that lies between the two minimums used to create it, the overbought line is created; and together they define an upward trend channel. This channel identifies a rising price.

The operator should be aware of overbought conditions. These conditions are created when the price exceeds the high end of the bullish channel. Due to too rapid an acceleration, the price reaches a point at which it is highly sensitive to long coverage and generally to the withdrawal of more experienced buyers, suggesting a weakening of the uptrend. They usually guide the price to a downward corrective action.

Human beings seem to be inclined towards extremes. In the financial markets this trend is revealed in the form of greed. Prices are pushed higher and higher until the public swells with stocks that are generally overvalued. When this happens, an overbought condition is said to exist.

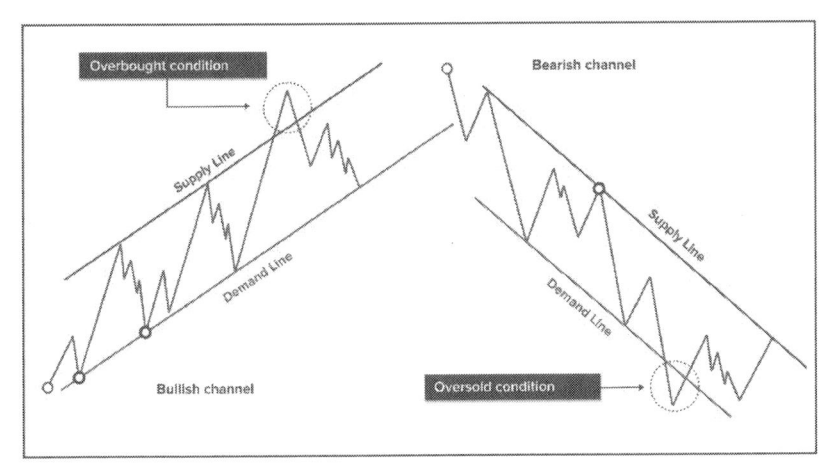

Channels

When the bearish trend line or supply line is dragged towards the opposite end and anchored parallel to the minimum that is located between the two maximums used for its creation, the oversold line is created; and together they define a bearish trend channel. This channel identifies a falling price.

The operator should be aware of overbooking conditions. These conditions are created when the price exceeds the low end of the downstream channel. Due to too fast a bearish movement, the price reaches a point at which it is highly sensitive to short coverage (profit taking) and a general withdrawal of experienced traders who were sold; suggesting a weakening of the bearish trend. They usually guide the price to an upward corrective action.

In a bear market there is another extreme that takes control; fear. As the price falls, traders become alarmed. The lower they go, the more frightened they get. Fear reaches a level that weak hands can't stand and sell their shares. This selling panic generates an overselling condition.

Those periods of overbought or overbought that lead to the stop of the movements can be seen in any temporality.

Inverted lines

In high-speed conditions where a clear trend has not yet been established, inverted lines are a good way to try to structure at least initially the price movement.

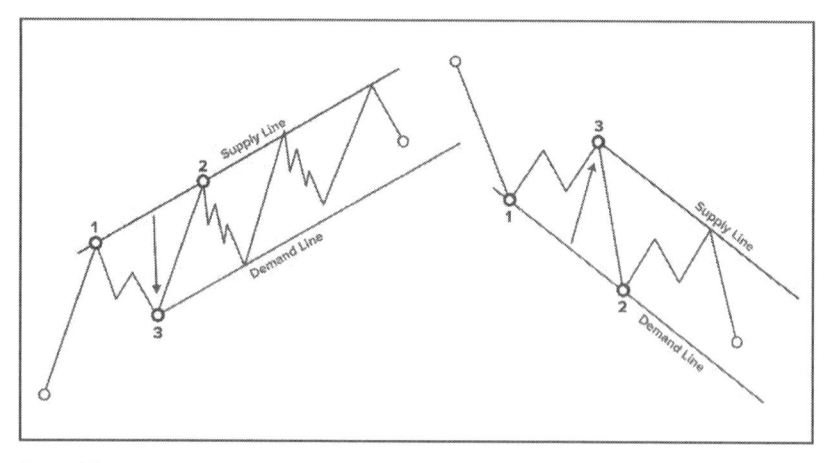

Inverted lines

It is a question of first creating the line of supply in an upward trend to generate from it the line of demand; and of first creating the line of demand in a downward trend to generate from it the line of supply.

At the beginning of a bullish advance, in case the price has made two important upward thrusts without leaving any significant bearish retreat, one can estimate at what point to expect the price to retreat by first creating the supply line in order to drag it and create the bullish trend line; and in the same way, first draw the demand line in order to create from it the bearish trend line.

Converging lines

There will be times when you will notice that overbought and oversold lines created from their trendlines do not work effectively. The price may never reach these lines as you will probably be following a different movement dynamic.

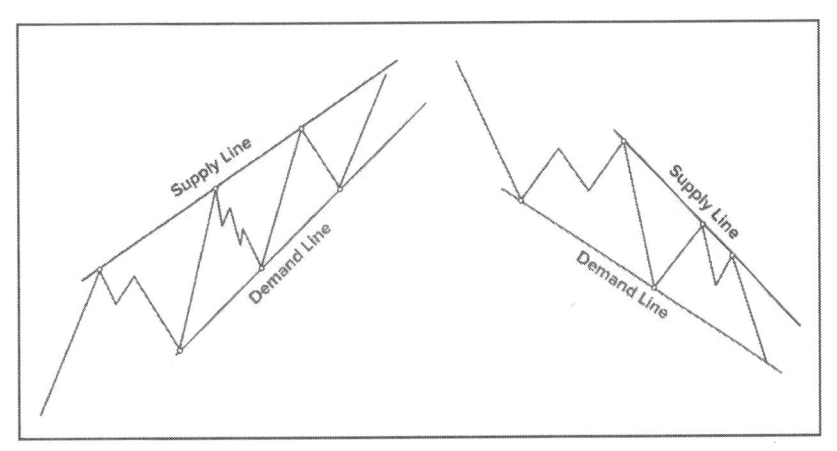

Converging lines

The way to solve this deficiency is to create these lines independently, without considering the trend line.

In this way, an overbought line would be created by connecting two maxima and the overbought line by connecting two minima. The objective is to try to find the structural logic to the movements in order to take advantage of them.

Note that in the case of an upward movement, not being able to even reach the original overbought line denotes a symptom of weakness and alerts us to a possible downward turn. Similarly, the fact that the original overbooking line cannot be reached in the case of the bear movement denotes a symptom of background strength and alerts us to a possible upward turn.

Visually they are observed as exhaustion patterns.

Chapter 5 – Trading Ranges

The market spends most of its time in this type of condition, so they are extremely important.

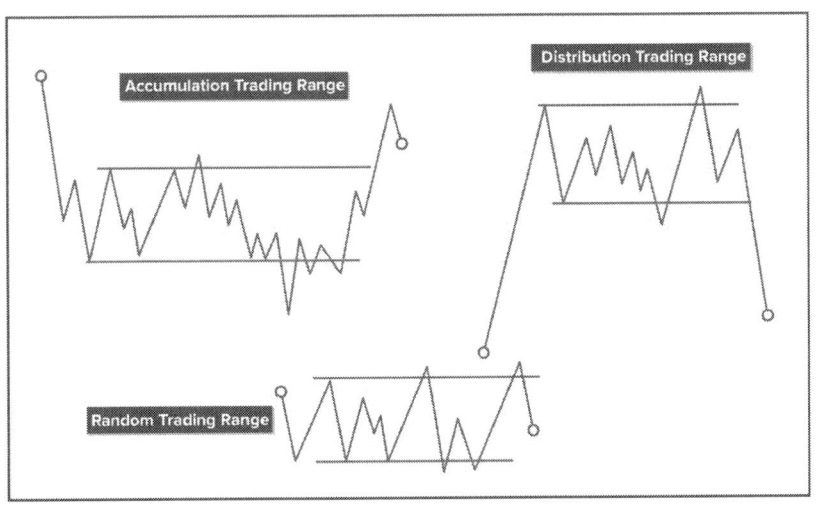

Types of Trading ranges

Trading ranges are places where previous movement has been stopped and there is a relative balance between supply and demand. It is within the range where accumulation or distribution campaigns are developed in preparation for an upward or downward trend. It is this force of accumulation or distribution that builds the cause that develops the subsequent movement.

The ranges within it present optimum trading opportunities with a very favourable risk/reward potential; however, large operations are those in which you correctly manage to position yourself within the range to take advantage of the trend movement.

In the operative in trend, as the price is already in movement, part of its path will have been lost. By taking advantage of opportunities within the range, there is a chance to catch a bigger move.

To be correctly positioned at the beginning of the trend, you must be able to analyze price action and volume during range development. Fortunately, the Wyckoff methodology offers unique guidelines with which the operator can successfully perform this task. The identification of events and the analysis of Phases become indispensable tools for the correct reading of the range.

If you don't see a clearly defined trend, the price is most likely in a range context. This neutral or lateral trend may have three main interests behind it: it is accumulating, in preparation for an upward movement; it is distributing, in preparation for a downward movement; or it is fluctuating up and down without any defined interest.

Random fluctuations should be ignored as there is probably no professional interest behind that market. It is important to understand that in not all trading ranges there is professional interest; and that therefore, if these interests are not involved in a security, the price simply fluctuates because it is in equilibrium and movements in one direction are neutralized with movements in the opposite direction.

On the basis of the law of cause and effect, it is necessary for the price to consume time within the range in preparation for the subsequent movement. And that movement will be directly proportional to the time spent in the range. This means that shorter ranges will generate shorter movements and that longer ranges will generate movements that will travel longer distances.

To define a range two points are required to build the channel. As long as the price remains within the range, no major movement will occur. The key is in the extremes. When these are broken, they can offer excellent trading opportunities.

Be clear that the decisive move to break the range and start the trend Phase cannot occur until a clear imbalance between supply and demand has been generated. At that point, the market must be in the control of the professionals and they must have confirmed that the direction in which they will direct the price movement is the path of least resistance.

This means that if they have accumulated with the intention of launching prices upwards, they will first verify that they will not find resistance (sales) to stop that rise. When they see that the road is clear, they will initiate movement. Similarly, if they have been distributing (selling) with the intention of lowering prices, they need to make sure that the floating demand (buyer interest) is relatively low.

Part 2 - The Wyckoff Method

Many of Wyckoff's basic principles have become basic foundations of technical analysis. The three fundamental laws: Supply and Demand, Cause and Effect and Effort and Result; the concepts of Accumulation/Distribution and the supremacy of Price and Volume when determining price movements are some examples.

The Wyckoff method has passed the test of time. More than 100 years of continuous development and use have proven the value of the method to trade all kinds of financial instruments.

This achievement should not come as a surprise as it relies on the analysis of price and volume action to judge how it reacts to the battle between the real forces that govern all price changes: supply and demand.

Chapter 6 - Wyckoff Methodology Structures

Financial markets are a living thing, they are constantly changing due to their continuous interaction between buyers and sellers. This is why it would be a mistake to use fixed patterns or schemes to try to read the context of the market.

Aware that it is practically impossible for price to develop two identical structures, the trading approach proposed by the Wyckoff methodology is flexible when analysing the market.

The price can develop different types of structures depending on the conditions in which it is found. This is why we need an approach that gives some flexibility to price movements but at the same time is governed by certain fixed elements that provide as much objectivity as possible to the reading.

These fixed aspects of the methodology are the events and Phases that make up the development of the structures. Below we present two basic schemes of accumulation and distribution to provide a very general idea of the dynamics in which price moves under the premises of the Wyckoff methodology.

As we have just said, these schemes can be considered as ideals. The important thing to keep in mind is that the market will not always present them this way.

Basic scheme of accumulation #1

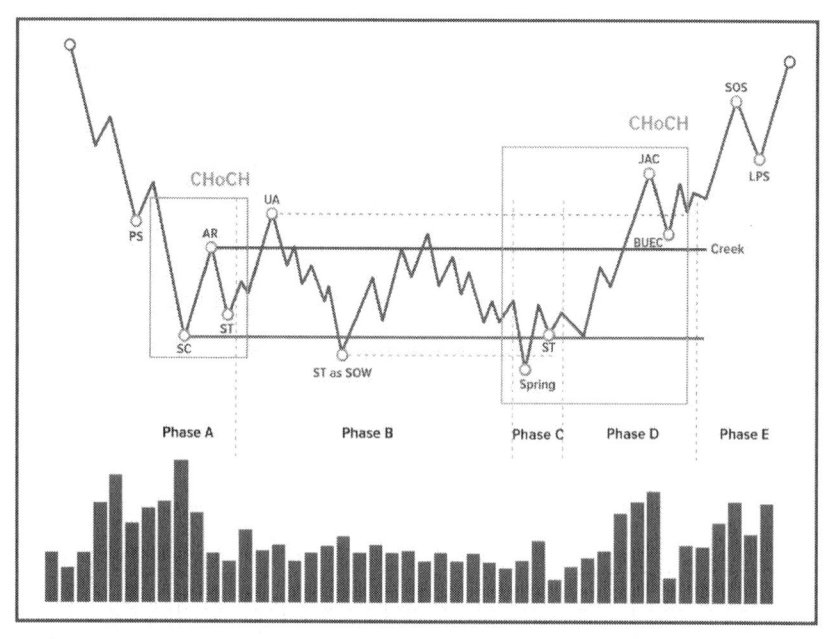

Basic scheme of accumulation #1

Accumulation. The process by which large operators absorb available stock from the market. This is a transfer from retail traders or "weak hands" to strong traders or "strong hands".

Creek. Resistance level for accumulation or reaccumulation structures. It is established by the maximum generated by the Automatic Rally and by the maximums that can be developed during Phase B.

CHoCH. Change of Character. It indicates the environment in which the price will move soon. The first CHoCH is established in Phase A where the price moves from a downward trend to a consolidation environment. The second CHoCH is set from the minimum of Phase C to the maximum of SOS in which the price moves from a consolidation environment to an upward trend environment.

Phase A. Stopping the previous bearish trend.

- **PS**. Preliminary Support. It's the first attempt to stop the downward movement that will always fail.
- **SC**. Selling Climax. Climate action that stops the downward movement.
- **AR**. Automatic Rally. Bullish reaction. An upward movement that sets the maximum range.
- **ST**. Secondary Test. Test of the level of supply in relation to climate action. Establishes the end of Phase A and the beginning of Phase B.

Phase B. Construction of the cause.

- **UA**. Upthrust Action. Temporary breakout of the resistance and re-entry into the range. This is a test at the maximum generated by the AR.
- **ST as SOW**. Secondary Test as Sign of Weakness. Sample of weakness in test function. Temporary break of the support and re-entry to the range. This is a test at the minimum generated by the SC.

Phase C. Test

- **SP Spring**. It is a test in the form of breakout of the minimums of Phases A and B. There are three different types of Springs.
- **Test Spring**. Downward movement towards lows of the range in order to check the commitment of the sellers.
- **LPS**. Last Point of Support. Test in the form of a bearish movement that fails to reach the minimum range.
- **TSO**. Terminal Shakeout or Shakeout. Abrupt movement of minimum breakout that produce a deep penetration of the level of support and a fast recovery.

Phase D. Bullish trend within the range.

- **SOS**. Sign of Strength. Bullish movement generated after the Phase C Test event that manages to reach the top of the range. Also called **JAC**. Jump Across the Creek. Creek jump.
- **LPS**. Last Point of Support. These are the rising troughs we find in the upward movement towards resistance.
- **BU**. Back Up. This is the last big reaction before the bull market starts. Also called **BUEC**. Back Up to the Edge of the Creek. Back to the creek.

Phase E. Bullish trend out of range. Succession of SOS and LPS generating a dynamic of rising highs and lows.

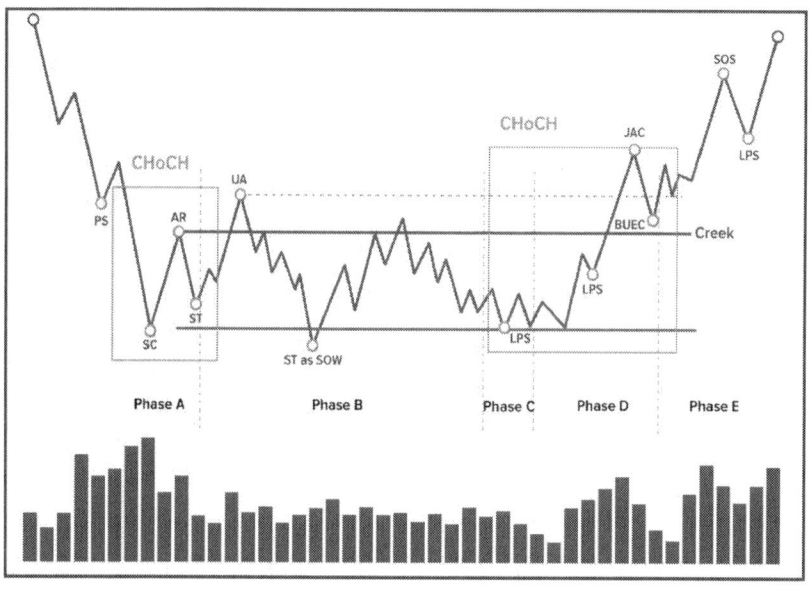

Basic scheme of accumulation #2

Basic scheme of accumulation #2

Second variant of the methodology in which the test event in Phase C fails to reach the minimums of the structure.

It usually occurs because current market conditions denote background strength.

The objective of the price is to visit this liquidity zone but the big operators support the market entering aggressively in purchase. They don't let the price go any lower so no one else can buy any lower.

This type of trading ranges is more complicated to identify because by not being able to assess that Shake action, the bullish approach loses a point of confidence.

The primary trading zone is in the Spring potential; then, when buying in a possible LPS we will always be in doubt if, as is most likely, the price will visit that minimum zone first to develop the Spring.

In addition to this, that first sign of bullish strength that produces range breakout is usually lost.

Therefore, the only viable purchase opportunity in this type of structure can be found in the BUEC. This is where we must pay more attention to look for entry in lengths.

Basic scheme of distribution #1

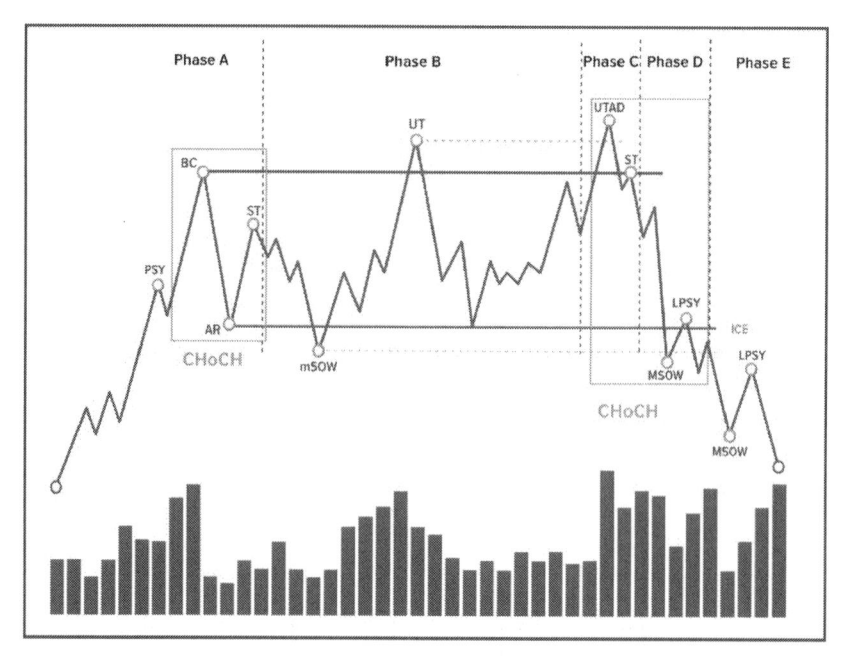

Basic scheme of distribution #1

Distribution. The process by which large operators distribute (sell) stock. This is a transfer from the strong operators or "strong hands" to the retail operators or "weak hands".

ICE. Level of support for distribution or redistribution structures. It is established by the minimum generated by the Automatic Reaction and by the minimums that can be developed during Phase B.

CHoCH. Change of Character. It indicates the environment in which the price will move soon. The first CHoCH is established in Phase A where the price moves from an upward trend environment to a consolidation environment. The second CHoCH is set from the maximum of Phase C to the minimum of the SOW in which the price moves from a consolidating environment to a downward trend environment.

Phase A. Stop the previous trend.

- **PSY**. Preliminary Supply. It's the first attempt to stop the climb that will always fail.
- **BC.** Buying Climax. Climate action that stops the upward movement.
- **AR.** Automatic Reaction. Bearish reaction. Bearish movement that sets the minimum range.
- **ST**. Secondary Test. Test of the level of demand in relation to climate action. Establishes the end of Phase A and the beginning of Phase B.

Phase B. Construction of the cause.

- **UT**. Upthrust. Same event as accumulation UA. Temporary breakout of the resistance and re-entry into the range. This is a test at the maximum generated by the BC.
- **mSOW**. Minor Sign of Weakness. Same event as ST as SOW of accumulation. Temporary break of the support and re-entry to the range. This is a test at the minimum generated by the AR.

Phase C. Test

1. **UTAD**. Upthrust After Distribution. It is a test in the form of breakout of the maximums of Phases A and B.
2. **UTAD test**. An upward movement that goes up to check the level of commitment of the buyers.

Phase D. Bearish Trend Within Range.

- **MSOW**. Major Sign of Weakness. Bearish movement originated after the Phase C Test event that manages to reach the bottom of the range generating a character change.
- **LPSY**. Last Point of Supply. These are the decreasing highs we find in the bearish movement towards support.

Phase E. Bearish trend out of range. Succession of SOW and LPSY generating a dynamic of diminishing maximums and minimums.

Basic scheme of distribution #2

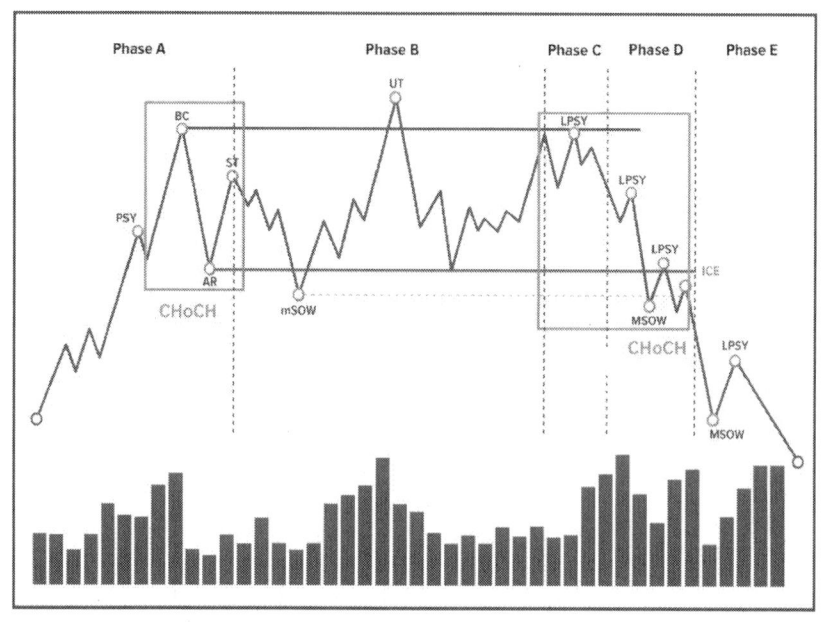

Basic scheme of distribution #2

Second variant of the methodology in which the test event in Phase C fails to reach the maximums of the structure.

Inverse reasoning than for the example of accumulation scheme #2.

Denotes a greater weakness in the background.

The price tries to reach the liquidity that there are in maximums but the big traders that are already short positioned prevent it,

Structures with a loss of confidence due to the absence of shaking. When going short on the possible LPSY we will always be in doubt as to whether the price will shake to highs before falling.

The sign of weakness (SOW) that breaks the structure is lost. Unique opportunity to the breakout test (LPSY).

Part 3 - The Three Fundamental Laws

Chapter 7 - The law of supply and demand

Richard Wyckoff was the first to introduce this fundamental law of economics and he told us that if demand was greater than supply, the price of the product would rise; that if supply was greater than demand, the price of the product would fall; and that if supply and demand were in equilibrium, the price of the product would be maintained.

This idea is very general and should be nuanced because there is a very common error in thinking that prices go up because there are more buyers than sellers or that they go down because there are more sellers than buyers.

In the market, there is always the same number of buyers and sellers; for someone to buy, there must be someone to sell to.

Theory

In the market, there are buyers and sellers who interrelate to match their orders. According to auction theory, the market seeks to facilitate this exchange between buyers and sellers; and this is why volume (liquidity) attracts price.

The general accepted theory in economics tells us that supply is created by sellers by placing sales (pending) limit orders in the ASK column and demand is created by buyers by placing purchase limit orders in the BID column.

There is a very common error in calling everything to do with the purchase demand and everything to do with the sale offer. Ideally, different terms should be used to distinguish between aggressive operators and passive operators.

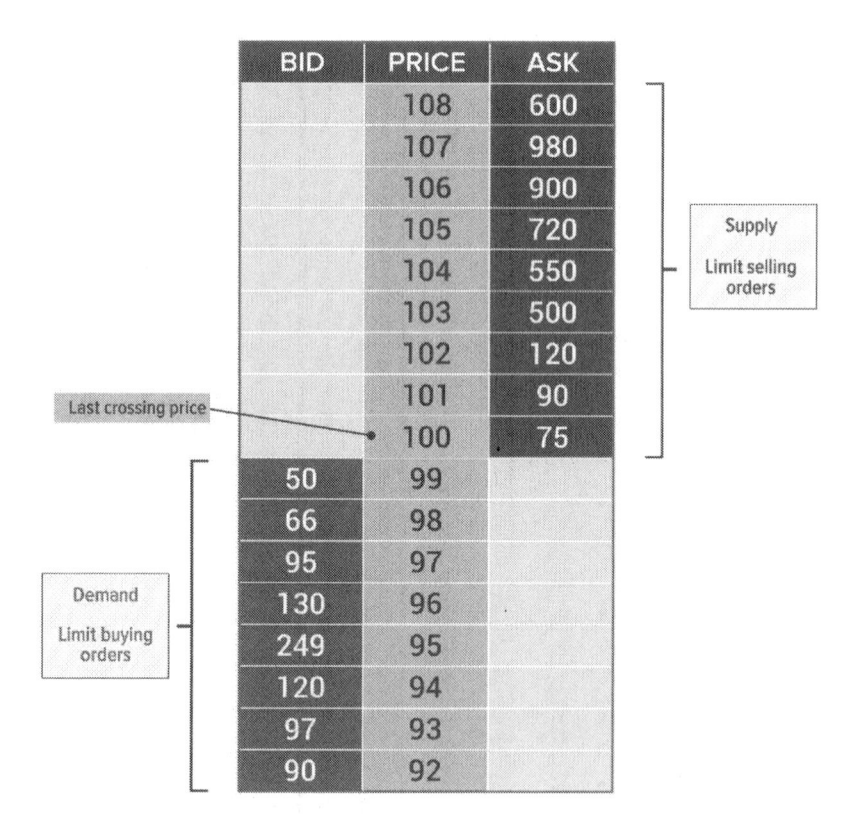

BID	PRICE	ASK
	108	600
	107	980
	106	900
	105	720
	104	550
	103	500
	102	120
	101	90
	100	75
50	99	
66	98	
95	97	
130	96	
249	95	
120	94	
97	93	
90	92	

Supply — Limit selling orders

Last crossing price → 100

Demand — Limit buying orders

Graphic Example of an Order Book

The terms supply and demand correspond to taking a passive attitude by placing limit orders in the BID and ASK columns.

While when an operator takes the initiative and goes to the BID column to execute an aggressive (to market) order, he is known as a seller; and when he goes to the ASK column, he is known as a buyer.

All this is a mere formality and has more to do with theory in economics than with practice. The key to everything is in the types of orders that are executed. We must differentiate between market orders (aggressive) and limit orders (passive).

Passive orders represent only intention, they have the capacity to stop a movement; but not the capacity to make the price move. This requires initiative.

Price shift

Initiative

In order for the price to move upwards, buyers have to buy all available sell orders at that price level and also continue to buy aggressively to force the price up one level and find new sellers there to trade with.

Passive buy orders cause the bearish movement to slow down, but on their own they cannot raise the price. The only orders that have the ability to move the price up are those purchases to market or those by whose crossing of orders becomes purchases to market.

Therefore, an upward movement of the price can be given by active entry of buyers or by executing Stop Loss of short positions.

BID	PRICE	ASK
	108	600
	107	980
	106	900
	105	720
	104	550
	103	500
	102	120
	101	90
	100	75
50	99	
66	98	
95	97	
130	96	
249	95	
120	94	
97	93	
90	92	

For the price to move up one leven, buyers must "eat" those 75 sell limit orders

For the price to move down one level, sellers must "eat" those 50 buy limit orders

Order book. Initiative

For the price to move downwards, sellers have to purchase all available purchase orders (demand) at that price level and continue to push downward by forcing the price to search for buyers at lower levels.

Passive sell orders cause the bullish movement to slow down, but it does not have the ability to bring the price down on its own. The only orders that have the ability to move the price down are sales to market or those by whose crossing of orders becomes sales to market.

Therefore, a downward movement of the price can be given by active entry of sellers or by executing Stop Loss of long positions.

BID	PRICE	ASK
	108	134
	107	100
	106	180
	105	120
	104	44
	103	26
	102	15
	101	7
	100	5
50	99	
66	98	
95	97	
130	96	
249	95	
120	94	
97	93	
90	92	

Large imbalance between buy and sell limit orders = lack of selling interest

Order book. Lack of interest

Lack of interest

It is also necessary to understand that the absence of one of the two forces can facilitate price displacement. An absence of supply can facilitate the rise in price just as an absence of demand can facilitate its fall.

When the bid is withdrawn, this lack of interest will be represented as a smaller number of contracts placed in the ASK column and therefore the price will be able to move more easily upwards with very little buying power.

Conversely, if demand is withdrawn, it will result in a reduction in the contracts that buyers are willing to place with the BID and this will cause the price to go down with very little selling initiative.

Conclusion

Regardless of the origin of the purchase or sale order (trader retail, institutional, algorithm and so on.) the result is that liquidity is added to the market; and this is what is really important when trading.

Two of the tools we can use to understand the result of this interaction between supply and demand are price and volume.

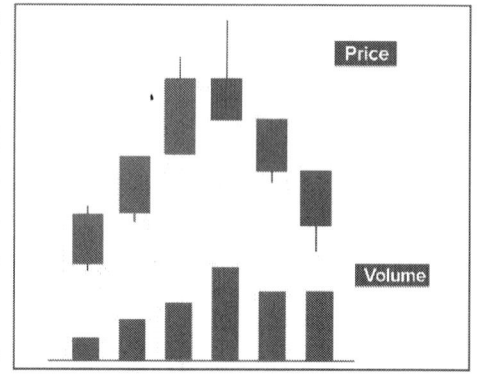

Price and Volume Graph

It is necessary to develop the ability to correctly interpret the price action with respect to its volume if we want to know at all times what is happening in the market.

This is why I consider the Wyckoff methodology to be a really solid approach when analyzing what is happening in the graph (accumulation and distribution processes) and making judicious scenarios.

Chapter 8 - The Law of Cause and Effect

The idea is that something cannot happen out of nowhere; that to see a change in price, a root cause must first have been built.

Generally, causes are constructed through a major change of hands between well-informed and uninformed operators.

In the case of individual transactions, the cause for the price to rise is the buyer's desire to want those shares or the seller's desire to want that money.

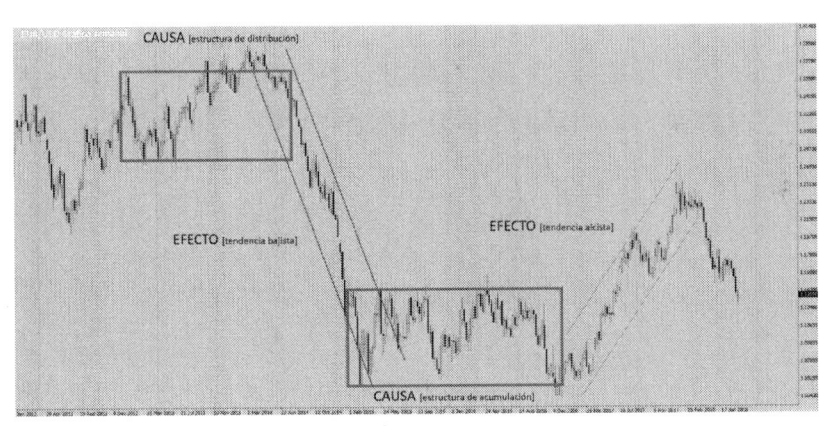

Weekly EUR/USD Chart. Example Cause/Effect

In addition to seeing the cause in terms of an individual operation, the objective is to see the cause from a broader perspective, in terms of movements. For this, it is said that the market is constructing a cause during periods of price lateralization; and that these generate later as an effect a trend movement to the rise or to the fall.

In these lateralization periods, stock absorption campaigns are carried out in which the big operators begin to position themselves on the right side of the market, gradually expelling the rest of the participants until they find the path on which the price will be directed free of resistance.

An important aspect of this law is that the effect realized by the cause will always be in direct proportion to that cause. Consequently, a great cause will produce a greater effect, and a small cause will result in a lesser effect.

It is logical to think that the longer the period of time the market spends in a rank condition developing a campaign, the greater the distance the subsequent trend movement will travel.

The key is to understand that it is during the lateral price Phases that the accumulation/distribution processes take place.

Depending on its duration and the efforts we see during its formation (manipulation manoeuvres such as shaking), this cause will provoke a response movement upwards or downwards (effect).

Elements to bear in mind

There are certain market conditions, such as climatic events, which can cause a sharp turn in the price without a great deal of preparation.

The big operators use these climate candles to accumulate/distribute all the stock they need without developing a more extensive campaign and starting from there the expected movement.

Another aspect to keep in mind is that not all ranges are accumulation or distribution processes. This point is very important.

Remember that the methodology tells us that there will be structures that are simply price fluctuations and do not have a motivating cause.

Point and Figure Graphics

In principle, the projection of the effect will be unknown, but we can propose it as proportional to the effort that provoked it.

Wyckoff used the point and figure graph to quantify cause and estimate effect.

By means of the horizontal counting of columns the possible objectives are estimated. It is about providing a good indication of how far a movement can go. Accumulation would produce an upward count while distribution would project it downward.

Unlike bar charts, which are time-based; point and figure charts are based on volatility.

In order for the dot and figure chart to advance to the right and generate a new column, it first requires a price movement in the opposite direction.

The count on this type of graph is made from right to left and is delimited between the two levels on which appeared first and lastly the force that controls the market at that time:

- For the projection of a count in an accumulation scheme we measure the number of columns between the Last Point of Support (last event on which the demand appears) and the Preliminary Support or Selling Climax (first events of appearance of the demand).
- For the projection of a distribution count we measure the number of columns between the Last Point of Supply and the Preliminary Supply or Buying Climax.

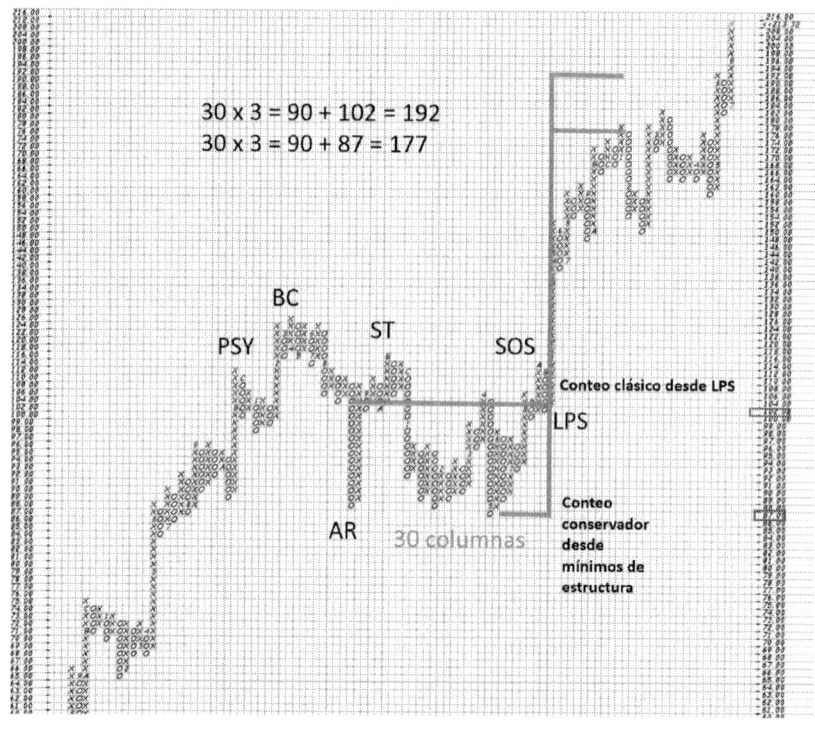

Example of counting in AAPL. Stockcharts.com Chart

    For the reaccumulation ranges the count is made from the Last Point of Support to the Automatic Reaction (as this is the first event on which the demand appeared).

- For the redistribution ranges the count is made from the Last Point of Support to the Automatic Rally (the first event on which the offer appeared).

    After counting the number of boxes that make up the range, the result is multiplied by the value of the box.

    The classic projection is obtained by adding the resulting figure to the price on which the LPS/LPSY is produced.

    To obtain a moderate projection, the resulting figure is added to the price of the highest extreme reached.

- In the distribution ranges, the highest maximum will generally be that set by the Upthrust (UT) or Buying Climax (BC).
- For the accumulation ranges, the lowest minimum will generally be the Spring (SP) or Selling Climax (SC).

Get a more conservative projection by dividing the area into Phases. Counts from and to where price turns occur. Count the number of boxes that make up each Phase and multiply it by the value of the box. The resulting figure is added to the price of the LPS/LPSY or to the price of the highest extreme reached.

Just because the value has ample preparation does not mean that the whole area is accumulation or distribution. This is why point and figure counts do not always reach the objective of greatest scope and therefore it is suggested to divide the range in order to generate several counts and thus establish different objectives.

Technical analysis for projection of objectives

There are operators who consider that the projection of targets by counting the point and figure graph is not very operative in today's markets.

There is also a problem with the point and figure at the time of its preparation because there are several ways to do it. This makes it useless from my point of view since this subjectivity makes me lose confidence in this tool.

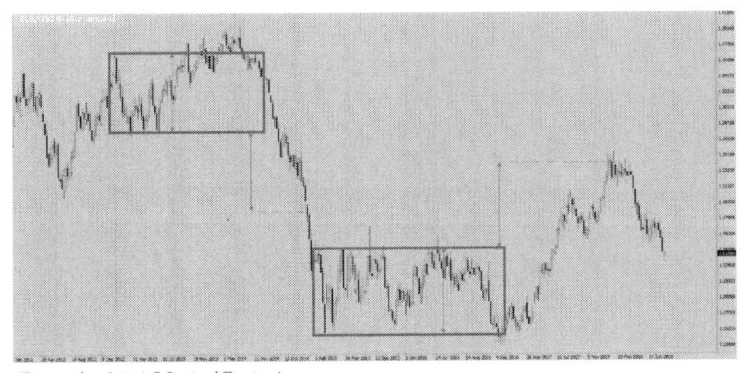

Example of 1:1 Vertical Projection

Some of us prefer to simplify it and use tools such as Fibonacci, Elliot or harmonic patterns (vertical projection of the range) for the projection of targets.

This type of tools is becoming more and more powerful since the inclusion of software in financial markets, many of the algorithms are programmed under these simple premises and therefore are objectives that are met with a high probability.

Conclusion

Since the market moves under this law of cause and effect by using the lateral Phases to generate the subsequent movements, I believe that it can give us an advantage to try to decipher what is "baking" during the development of these structures.

And to try to figure out what's going on there, the Wyckoff methodology gives us excellent tools.

Wyckoff traders know that it is in these lateral conditions from where the movements are born and that is why we are continuously looking for the beginning of new structures to begin to analyze the action of price and volume with the objective of positioning ourselves before the development of the trend movement.

A trend will end and a cause will begin. A cause will end and a trend will begin. The Wyckoff method is centered around the interpretation of these conditions.

Chapter 9 - The Law of Effort and Result

In financial markets, effort is represented by volume while the result is represented by price.

This means that the price action must reflect the volume action. Without effort, it can't have worked.

The aim is to assess the dominance of buyers or sellers through convergence and divergence between price and volume.

The importance of volume

Price is not the only important factor in financial markets. Perhaps even more important is the character of the volume.

These two elements (price and volume) are part of the cornerstone of the Wyckoff methodology.

Volume identifies the amount of stock (stocks, units, contracts) that has changed hands. When large traders are interested in a security, this will be reflected in the volume traded.

This is the first key concept: the participation of large operators is identified by an increase in volume.

Harmony and divergence

A significant increase in volume indicates the presence of professional money with the aim of producing a movement (continuation or spin).

If the effort is in harmony with the result it is a sign of strength of the movement and suggests its continuation. If the effort is in divergence with the result it is a sign of weakness of the movement and suggests a reversal.

It should also be noted that the price movement will be in direct proportion to the amount of effort expended.

If harmony is suggested, a greater effort will cause a movement of long duration; while a slight effort will be reflected in a movement of shorter duration.

On the other hand, if divergence is suggested, the result tends to be in direct proportion to that divergence. A smaller divergence tends to generate a smaller result and a larger divergence, a larger result.

Analysis table

Suggestion	In the development of a candle	On the next scroll	In the development of the movements	By waves	By reaching key levels
Harmony	High volume developing a wide range	High volume in a bullish candle that makes the price rise	High volume in an impulse	Increasing wave in an impulse	High volume breaking level
Harmony	Low volume developing a narrow range	High volume in a bearish candle that lowers the price	Low volume in a pullback	Decreasing wave in a pullback	Low volume that does not break the level
Divergence	High volume developing a narrow range	High volume in a bullish candle that does not raise the price	Low volume in an impulse	Decreasing wave in an impulse	High volume that does not break the level
Divergence	Low volume developing a wide range	High volume in a bearish candle that does not bring down the price	High volume in a pullback	Increasing wave in a pullback	Low volume breaking level

Summary Analysis Table Effort/Result

The complete table of harmony/divergence at the time of evaluating the action of the price and the volume is the following one:

In the development of a candle

It's the simplest evaluation. We try to analyze the price and volume action in a simple individual candle.

Candles are the final representation of a battle between buyers and sellers within a certain period of time.

The final result of this interaction between supply and demand sends us a message.

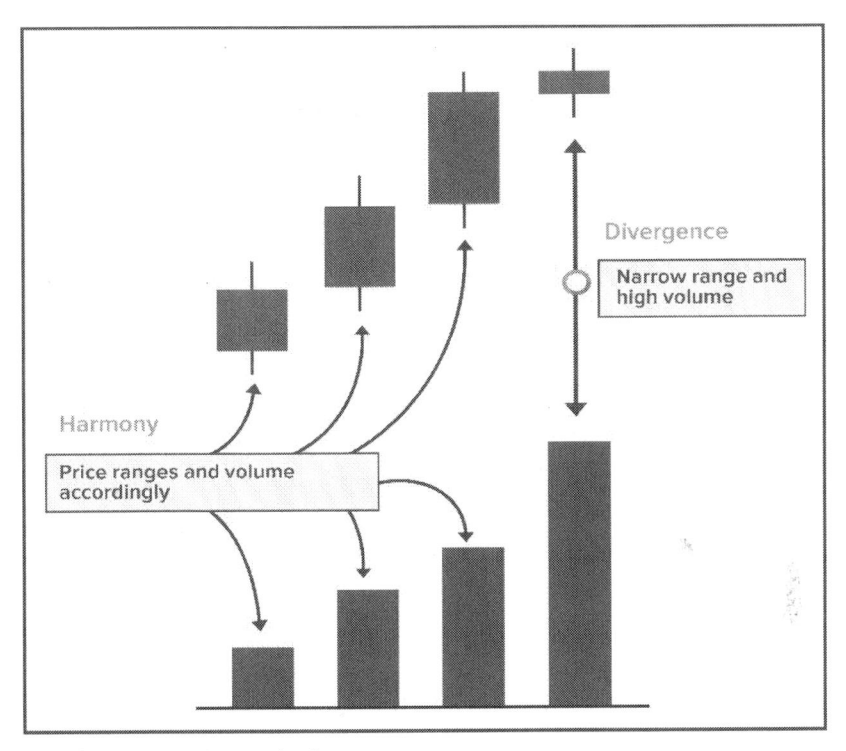

Effort/Result in Developing a Candle

Our job as traders who analyze the action of price and volume is to know how to interpret that message correctly. In this case in isolation.

We are looking for an agreement between the price ranges and the volume traded. For that message to convey harmony, we want to see wide ranges in the volume peaks and narrow ranges in the low volumes. The opposite would mark a divergence.

On the next scroll

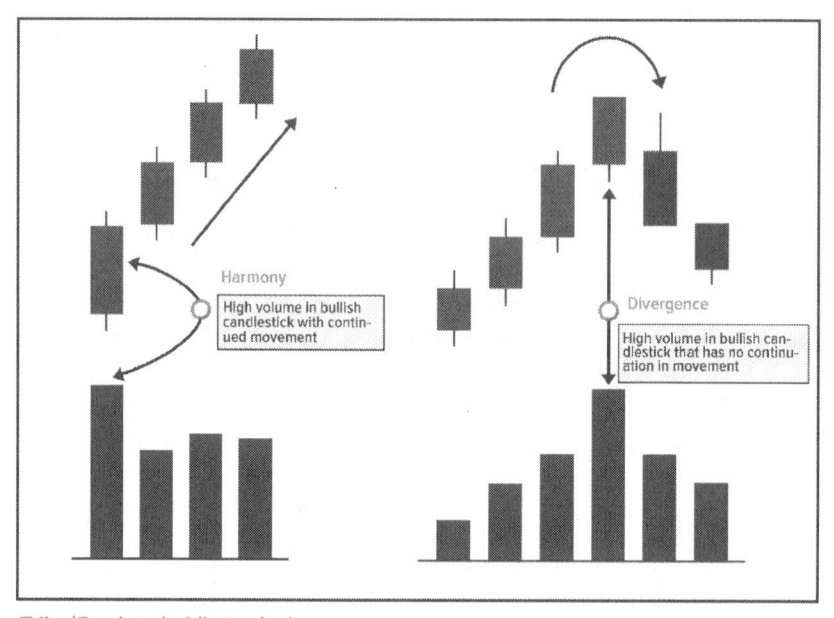

Effort/Result in the following displacement

In this section, we try to analyze the action of the price and the volume in a larger portion; in the later displacement of the price.

We want to assess whether this volume generates a movement in the direction of the original candle or whether the price shifts in the opposite direction after observing this increase in volume.

Therefore, we would obtain a harmony effort/result if that candle + that volume have continuation; and divergence if a turn is generated in the market.

In the development of the movements

We increase the portion of our analysis and on this occasion, we analyze the price action and the volume in term of complete movements.

As a general rule, impulse movements will be accompanied by an increase in volume as the price moves in the direction of least resistance; and backward movements will be accompanied by a decrease in volume.

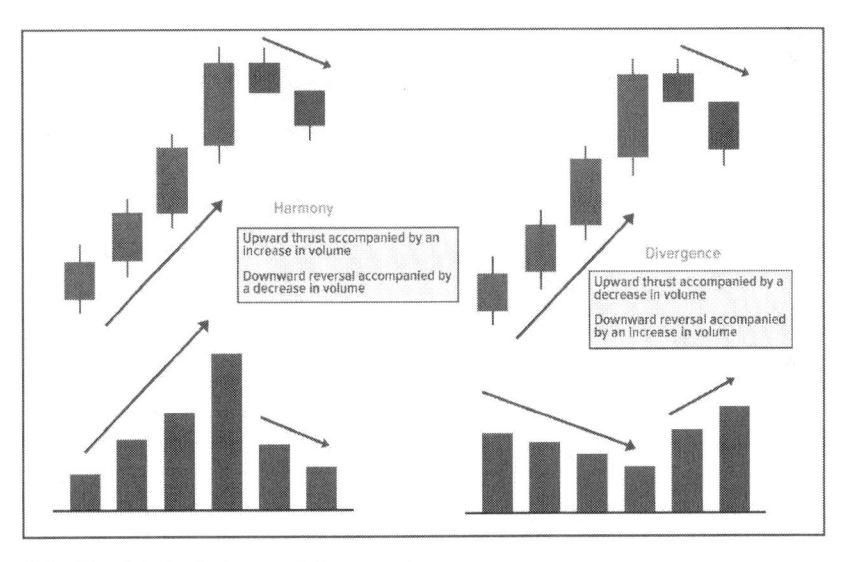

Effort/Result in the development of the movements

Then, we determine that there is harmony when an impulse comes with increased volume; and when a retreat comes with decreased volume.

Similarly, we determine divergence when we observe an impulsive movement (which generates a new maximum/minimum) with a decrease in volume and when we see a retrocession (we would have to evaluate if it is really a retrocession) with an increase in volume.

By Waves

This tool (originally created by David Weis) measures the volume that has been operated by each wave (up and down).

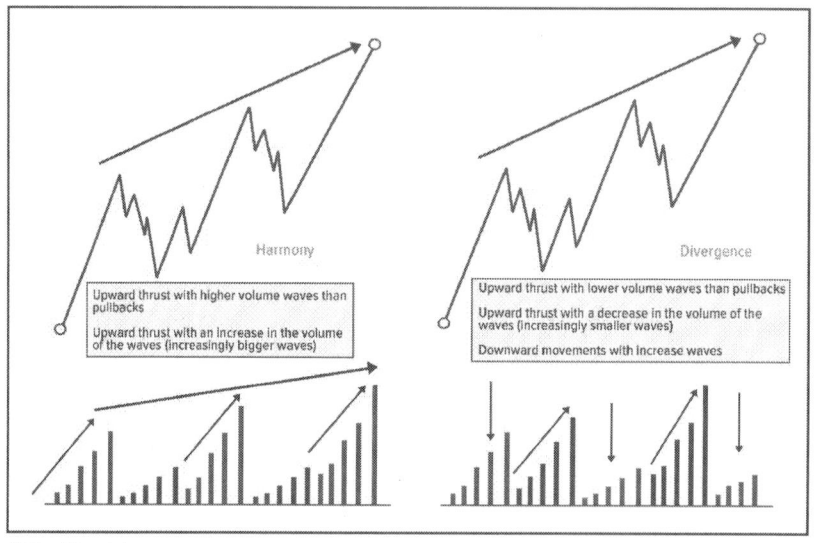

Effort/Result by waves

Overall, it allows us to assess market conditions and more accurately compare upward and downward pressure between moves.

A key fact to keep in mind when analyzing the waves is that not all the volume traded on a bullish wave will be purchases and that not all the volume traded on a bearish wave will be sales.

Like any other element, it requires analysis and interpretation. The analysis of effort and result is exactly the same.

It is a question of comparing the current wave of volume with the previous ones; as much with the one that points in its direction as with the one that goes in the opposite direction.

Harmony would be obtained if in an upward movement, the upward impulses are accompanied by upward waves with a greater volume than the downward setbacks.

We would also determine a harmony if the price reaches new highs and each bullish impulse does so with an increase in the volume of the waves.

On the other hand, we would have a divergence if the price moves upwards but the rising waves are less and less; or if in that moving upwards the falling waves show greater strength.

By reaching key levels

It is one more way to evaluate this law of effort and result; this time, in terms of broken levels.

It is simple: if you approach a level with volume and make an effective break we will say that there is harmony effort/result in that breakout movement. That volume was intended to move forward and has absorbed all the orders that were placed there.

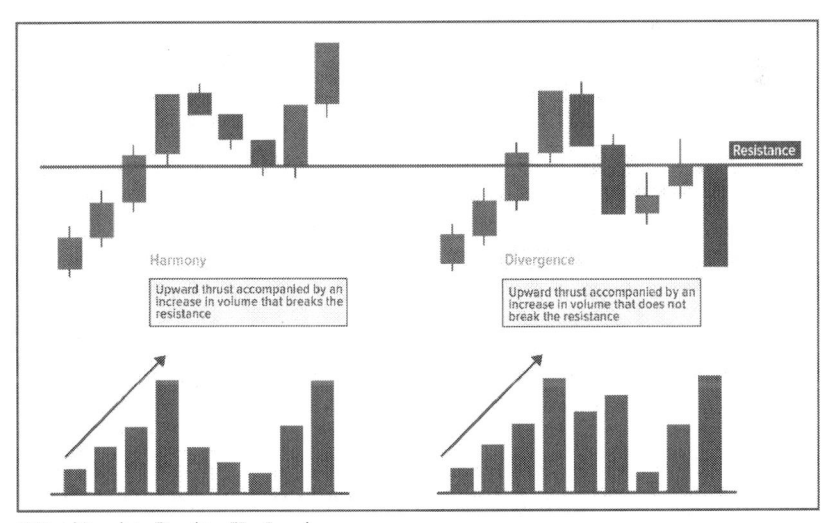

Effort/Result in Reaching Key Levels

If, on the other hand, you approach a level with volume and make a false break, we will say that there is divergence. All of that operated volume has been participating in the opposite direction to the level break.

It can be applied to any type of level. Whether horizontal (supports and resistances), with slope (trend lines, channel lines, inverted lines, converging, diverging), dynamic levels (moving averages, VWAP, bands); as well as any other level that establishes a specific methodology.

Effort/Result in Trends

In addition to what was previously studied, the evaluation of the effort/result can be included in other more general market contexts such as trends.

Generally, large relative volumes accompany the termination of a large movement, especially if accompanied by small price advances.

Therefore, a strong volume after a strong bearish trend indicates that the fall is almost complete. It may be a sales climax and you're probably starting an accumulation.

Similarly, a strong volume after a prolonged uptrend indicates that the end of the uptrend is near and that the distribution Phase may be beginning.

Lack of interest

Turns do not always occur when there is a considerable volume (effort) and a comparatively small price movement (result).

We find another way capable of causing a price twist; and that is lack of interest. Small volumes on market floors (after a considerable decline), or after a bearish reversal, generally indicate lack of selling pressure.

If there is no interest in continuing to fall, an appearance of buyers now would cause a turn upside. Similarly, small volumes on market ceilings (after a considerable rise) or after a bullish retreat, usually indicate lack of buying pressure that would lead the price to a bearish turn with the appearance of sellers.

Remember that sudden relative increases or decreases in volume are significant and will help you identify when a movement may be ending or about to end.

Part 4 - The processes of accumulation and distribution

Chapter 10 - Accumulation

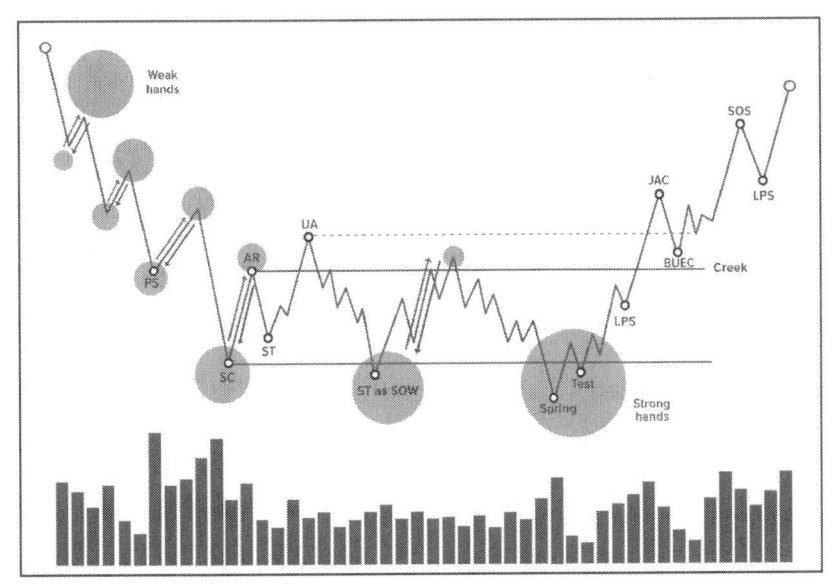

Stock Exchange in Accumulation

An accumulation range is a lateral movement of the price preceded by a bearish movement on which an absorption manoeuvre is carried out by the big operators with the objective of accumulating stock in order to be able to sell it at higher prices in the future and make a profit from the difference.

Stock control

During the development of the bearish movement that precedes it, control of the stock will be mainly in weak hands. In order to be able to turn a market, it is necessary for that stock to be controlled by the great professionals, by the strong hands.

As the price falls, the stock gradually changes hands; the more it falls, the greater the stock is in strong positions. It is during the development of the accumulation structure that the final process of absorption takes place. The moment at which the price is ready to start the upturn.

The law of cause and effect

It is in these range conditions where we see in operation the law of cause and effect in trading; which tells us that for there to be an effect, there must first be a cause that originates it; and that the effect will be in direct proportion to the cause.

In the case of the accumulation range, the purchase of stock (cause) will have the effect of a subsequent upward trend movement; and the extent of this movement will be in direct proportion to the time the price has spent building that cause (absorbing the stock).

The preparation of an important movement takes considerable time. A big trader can't buy everything he wants all at once because if he executes an order with all the quantity he wants, he would get worse prices due to the displacement his own order would generate.

In order to perform this task, professionals need to plan and execute a careful plan with which to try to absorb all available stock at the lowest possible average price.

Handling maneuvers

In the accumulation process, large operators create an environment of extreme weakness. The news at this point is likely to be bad and many will be influenced to enter the wrong side of the market. By means of various manoeuvres, they manage to make themselves little by little with all the available offer.

In the accumulation range we observe a fundamental event that characterizes this type of context since in many occasions it is the action that initiates the trend movement. It's the bearish shake, also known as "Spring" It is a sudden downward movement which breaks the support level of the range and with which the big traders are used to carry out a triple function: To reach the stop loss of those traders who were well positioned on the long side; to induce for sale the ill-informed traders who think in the continuation of the downward movement; and to profit from such movement.

While it is true that this shaking event is an action that adds strength to the bullish scenario, it is also true that it will not always happen. You should be aware that on many occasions the development of the uptrend will begin without this terminal action. This is a context that is somewhat more difficult to determine but equally valid.

At the same time, they need to take the "weak hands" out of the market. These are traders who, if they are positioned to buy, will very soon close their positions assuming short profits; and this closing of buy positions are sales orders that the big traders will have to keep absorbing if they want to keep pushing the price. One action they take to get rid of this type of weak operator is to generate a flat, boring market context in order to discourage these operators from finally closing their positions.

Counterparty, liquidity

Both the fact of reaching the stops of the purchase positions, as well as the entry in sale of some operators, provides liquidity to the professionals that are accumulating; since both actions execute sales to market; and these sales are the counterpart that the big operators need to marry their purchases.

In addition to this, when the bullish reversal occurs back into the range, stops will also be executed for those who entered with selling positions during the bearish break, adding strength to the bullish movement.

The path of least resistance

Professionals with interests above will not initiate the movement until they have verified that the path of least resistance is on the rise. This is achieved by carrying out various tests to check the level of commitment of the sellers.

As with Spring, they will initiate downward movements to verify the tracking it has. An absence of volume at this point would suggest a lack of interest in reaching lower prices.

This is why sometimes you see more than one Shake within the range; these are tests that professionals develop to make sure they won't find resistance at higher prices.

Common characteristics of the accumulation ranges

The following are key features of the accumulation ranges:

- **Decrease in volume and volatility as the range develops.** There will be less and less stock available for sale and therefore price and volume fluctuations will be gradually reduced.
- **Tests to the high zone of the range without volume**, suggesting an absence of selling interest; except when the price is prepared to initiate the movement out of the range.
- **Springs to previous lows**; either over the support area or over minor lows within the range.
- **Wider and smoother upward movements and bars than bearishists**. This denotes an influx of good quality demand and suggests that supply is of poor quality.
- **Development of rising highs and lows**. This sequence should already be observed in the last stage of the range, just before the start of the bullish jump. Denotes total control by buyers.

Beginning of the bullish movement

When there is no longer any stock to be absorbed, a turning point takes place. Value control is in the hands of the strong and they will only get rid of their positions at much higher prices. A slight increase in demand now would provoke a sudden upward movement in prices, initiating the upward trend.

Chapter 11 - Reaccumulation

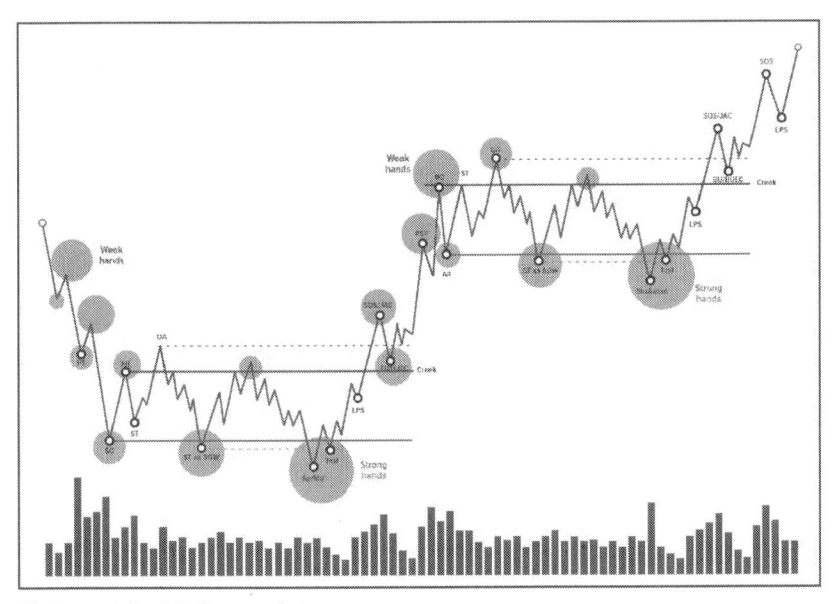

Exchange of Stock in Reaccumulation

The reaccumulation process is exactly identical to the accumulation process. The only difference between the two is the way the structure begins to develop. While the accumulation range begins by stopping a bearish movement, the reaccumulation range begins after the stop of an upward movement.

Stock Absorption

A reaccumulation is the result of a previous uptrend that needs to be consolidated. The hands that control the value will change during the course of the trend.

At the beginning of an uptrend, the value is under the control of very strong owners (professional traders, strong hands), but as it develops, the stock will gradually shift to less informed operators, weak hands.

At this point, it is said that the demand is of poor quality and the market needs to restart a process of stock absorption in which again it is the big operators who take control.

Duration of the structure

A key point to keep in mind is that the duration of this structure will be influenced by the percentage of strong and weak hands that have control of the value.

If at the beginning of the reaccumulation the value is still mainly in strong hands, the duration of the structure will be shorter. If, on the other hand, it is the weak hands that control most of the stock, a longer period of time will be necessary to be able to redevelop the purchasing process.

The objectives of the main accumulation will not yet be met and this structure is developed to add new demand to the market with which to continue the upward movement towards these objectives.

Reaccumulation or Distribution

A judicious analysis of price and volume action is very important in order not to make the mistake of confusing a reaccumulation range with a distribution range.

Both are initiated in the same way, after the stop of an upward movement. It becomes necessary to automate the characteristics of the accumulation ranges, as this is one of the most compromising situations that any Wyckoff operator will encounter.

Chapter 12 - Distribution

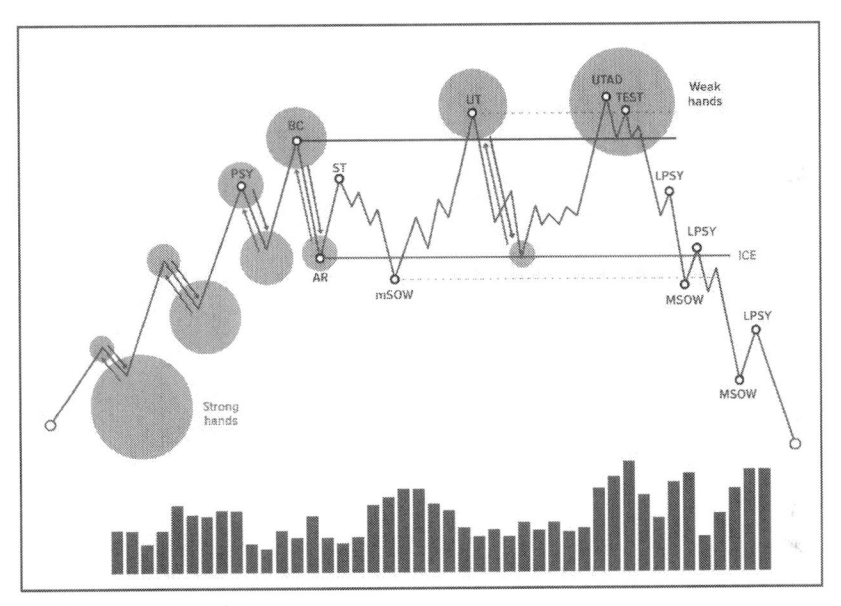

Stock Exchange in Distribution

A distribution range is a lateral movement of the price which manages to stop an upward movement and in which there is a process of selling stock by well-informed professionals, who have interests at lower prices. They try to store a great position in order to get rid of it at lower prices and get a return for it.

The law of cause and effect

It is in these range conditions where we see in operation the law of cause and effect so cooked in the world of trading; which tells us that for there to be an effect, there must first be a cause that originates it; and that the effect will be in direct proportion to the cause.

In the case of the distribution range, the sale of stock (cause) will have the effect of a subsequent downward trend movement; and the extent of this movement will be in direct proportion to the time the price has spent building that cause (absorbing the stock).

The preparation of an important movement takes considerable time. A large trader cannot build his entire position at once because if he executes his sell orders with an order containing all the quantity he wants; the very aggressiveness of the order would shift the price downwards until he finds the necessary demand with which to match his sell orders and this would lead to worse prices.

In order to perform this task, professionals need to develop and carry out a careful plan with which to try to absorb all available market demand at the highest possible average price.

Handling maneuvers

During this distribution process, the large operators, supported by the media (often at their service) generate an environment of extreme strength. What they are looking for with this is to attract as many traders as possible since it will be the purchases of these traders who will give the necessary counterpart to match their sales orders.

Misinformed traders don't know that strong professionals are building a great selling position because they have interests below. You'll be entering the wrong side of the market. By means of various manoeuvres, they are able to make themselves little by little with all the available demand.

In the distribution range, as in the accumulation range, we will be presented with the fundamental event of the shock. While it is true that not all structures will see this action before starting the trend movement, the fact of its presence adds great strength to the scenario.

In the case of a bullish shock, the Wyckoff methodology calls it "Upthrust". This is a sudden upward movement which breaks the resistance level of the range and with which large traders are used to carry out a triple function: Reach the stops loss of those traders who were well positioned on the short side; induce in buy to ill-informed traders who think in the continuation of the bullish movement; and profit from such movement.

At the same time, they need to take the "weak hands" out of the market. These are traders who, if positioned for sale, will very soon close their positions assuming short profits; and this closing of sale positions are buy orders that the big traders will have to keep absorbing if they want to keep pushing the price. One action they take to get rid of this type of weak operator is to generate a flat, boring market context in order to discourage these operators from finally closing their positions.

Counterparty, liquidity

The professionals who are building their position are obliged to carry out this type of manoeuvre. Due to the magnitude of their positions, it is the only way they have to be able to operate in the markets. They need liquidity with which to match their orders and the jerk event is a great opportunity to get it.

The stop jumping of sell positions, as well as traders entering long, are buy orders that must necessarily be crossed with a sell order. And indeed, it is the well-informed traders who are placing those sales orders and thus absorbing all the purchases that are executed.

In addition, when the bearish reversal occurs after the shake, the stops of those who bought will also be executed, adding strength to the bearish movement.

The path of least resistance

Once the development of the range is coming to an end, the great professionals will not initiate the downward trend movement until they can verify that effectively the path of least resistance is down.

They do this through tests with which they evaluate the buyer's interest. They initiate upward movements and depending on the second participation (this will be observed by the volume traded in that movement) they will value if demand remains available or if on the contrary, the buyers are exhausted. An absence of volume at this point would suggest a lack of interest in reaching higher prices.

This is why you sometimes see more than one Shake in the range; these are tests that professionals develop to make sure they won't find resistance at lower prices.

Common characteristics of the distribution ranges

The following are key characteristics of the distribution ranges:

- **High volume and volatility during range development**. Wide price fluctuations will be observed and the volume will remain relatively high and constant.
- **Tests to the lower zone of the range without volume**, suggesting an absence of buyer interest; except when the price is prepared to initiate the movement out of the range.
- **Upward Shakes to previous highs**; either over the resistance area or over minor highs within the range.

- **Wider and more fluid movements and down bars than up movements and up bars**. This denotes entry of quality supply and suggests that demand is of poor quality.
- **Development of decreasing maximums and minimums**. This sequence should already be observed in the last stage of the range, just before the start of the bearish jump. What he's suggesting is that the bearishists are being more aggressive.

Beginning of the Bearish Movement

When demand is no longer available, a turning point takes place. Value control is in the hands of the strong and they will only get rid of their positions at much lower prices. A slight increase in supply now would provoke a sharp downward movement in prices, initiating the downward trend.

Chapter 13 - Redistribution

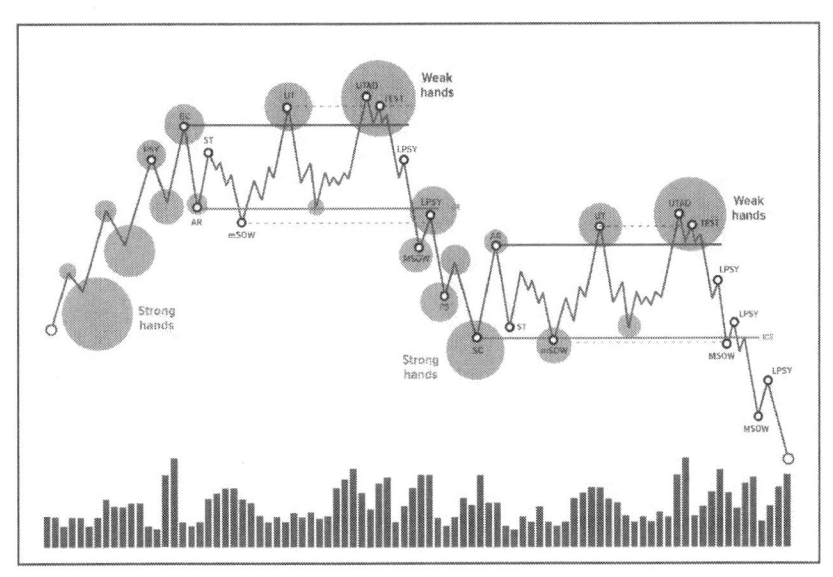

Stock Exchange in Redistribution

The redistribution Phase is a range that comes from a bearish trend and is followed by a new bearish trend. Multiple Phases of redistribution can occur within a large bear market. This is a pause that refreshes the value to develop another downward movement.

Redistribution or accumulation

This type of structure starts the same as the accumulation ranges; therefore, a very judicious analysis is necessary in order not to lead to erroneous conclusions. This aspect is undoubtedly one of the most difficult tasks for the Wyckoff operator: to know how to distinguish between a redistribution range and an accumulation range.

Stock control

During the periods of redistribution, the great professional who is already short returns to sell around the top of the range and potentially cover (close/buy) some of his positions near the base of the range.

In general, they are increasing the size of their short position during range development. The reason they close some of their short positions at the base of the range is to provide price support and not to push it down prematurely before they can establish a significant short position.

Redistribution remains volatile during and at the end of its development before continuing the downtrend.

The hands that control the value will change during the course of the trend. At the beginning of a bearish trend, the value is under the control of very strong owners (professional traders, strong hands), but as it develops, the stock will gradually change towards less informed operators, weak hands. At this point, it is said that the supply is of poor quality and the market needs to restart a process of stock absorption in which again it is the big operators who take control.

Duration of the structure

The percentage of strong and weak hands that have control of the value will influence the duration of the structure. If at the beginning of the redistribution the value is still mainly in strong hands, the duration of the structure will be shorter. If, on the other hand, it is the weak hands that control most of the stock, a longer period of time will be necessary to be able to redevelop the sales process.

The objectives of the main distribution will not yet be met and this structure is being developed to add new selling positions to the market with which to continue the downward movement towards these objectives.

Part 5 - Events

The Wyckoff methodology attempts to identify logical patterns of price turn during which market control is defined.

In this section, we will present the sequence that follows the price in the development of these structures. Although there are operators who apply it differently, from my point of view it is advisable to observe such events from a practical point of view, subtracting rigidity and providing as much flexibility as possible to the analysis.

The events are the same for both cumulations and distributions. The only thing that changes in some cases is the name, but the underlying logic behind them is the same. We will divide the sections by events and within them we will explain both the example of upward and downward turns.

The list of events

Although they will be further developed later, we make a brief summary of the logic of each of the events that will appear:

Event #1: Preliminary Stop

The preliminary stop is the first attempt to stop the trend movement underway, the result of which will always fail. It is an early warning that the trend may be coming to an end.

Event nº2: Climax

This is the culmination movement of the preceding trend. After having covered a great distance, the price will reach an extreme condition that will provoke the appearance of the great professional.

Event nº3: Reaction

It is the first great signal that suggests the change of sentiment in the market. We go from a market in control by either of the two forces to a market in equilibrium.

Event nº4: Test

This event has different readings depending on the location where it takes place. In general terms, it tries to evaluate the commitment or absence of it on the part of the operators in a certain moment and direction.

Event nº5: Shaking

Key moment for the structure analysis. It is the last deception developed by the professional before initiating the tendential movement in favor of the least resistance.

Event nº6: Breakout

It is the greatest proof of commitment that the professional has to assume. If you have done a good previous work of absorption, you will break relatively easily the structure in order to continue the movement out of it.

Event #7: Confirmation

If the analysis is correct, a rupture test will be developed which will confirm that the professional is positioned in that direction and supports the movement.

Chapter 14 - Event #1: Preliminary Stop

This is the first Wyckoff method event that appears to initiate the Phase A stop of the previous trend.

In the case of accumulation schemes, it is called Preliminary Support (PS), which together with the Selling Climax (SC), the Automatic Rally (AR) and the Secondary Test (ST) produces the change in character with which it makes the price evolve from a downward trend environment to a lateralisation environment.

In the example of the distribution structures it is called Preliminary Supply (PSY), which in conjunction with the Buying Climax (BC), the Automatic Reaction (AR) and the Secondary Test (ST), puts an end to Phase A, stopping the previous upward trend and initiating Phase B, the construction of the cause.

As we know, the processes of accumulation and distribution require time and on rare occasions the price will develop a hypodermic scheme visually leaving a V turn. This accumulation process begins with this first event, with Preliminary Support and Preliminary Supply.

Before this event takes place, the market will find itself in a clear trend. At some point, the price will reach a level attractive enough for large traders that they will begin to participate more aggressively.

How the preliminary stop appears on the graphic

The observation of this event on the graph is generally misinterpreted as it is not necessarily necessary to observe a bar with increased volume and expansion in the ranges.

It can also be seen on a set of bars with a relatively narrower range and a constant high volume during all of them; or even on a single bar with a high volume and a large wick. These representations in the end denote the same thing: the first relevant entry of the big operators.

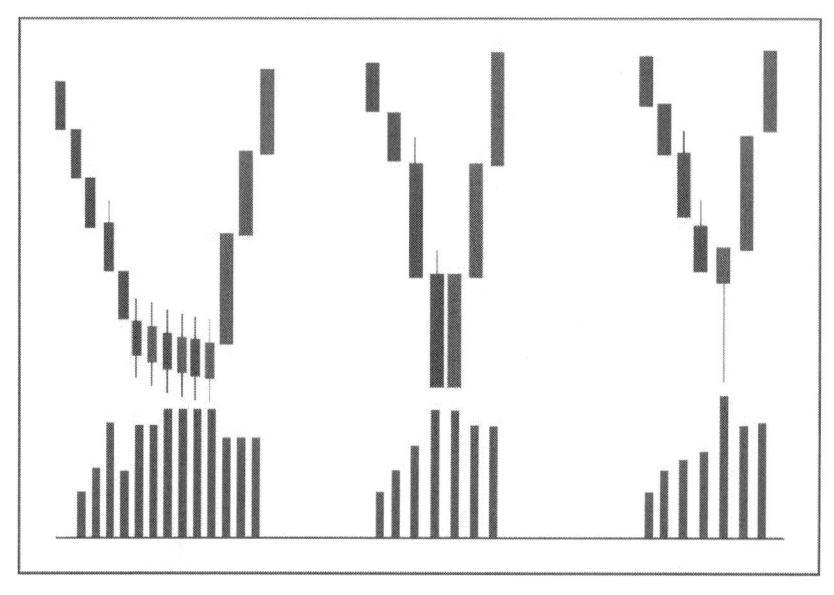

Visualization of Bullish Rotation with Large Volume

He recalls one of the most important quotes from Tom Williams' book *Master the Markets* in which he says something like that the market does not like large trend bars with significant volume increase after a prolonged move as they usually denote an opposite sentiment.

Observing a large bearish bar with a peak of volume and closing at minimums after a prolonged downward movement is a very clear indication of professional buying.

It is likely that this stock will reach an oversold condition in relation to the bearish channel that is respecting the price stock during the bearish movement.

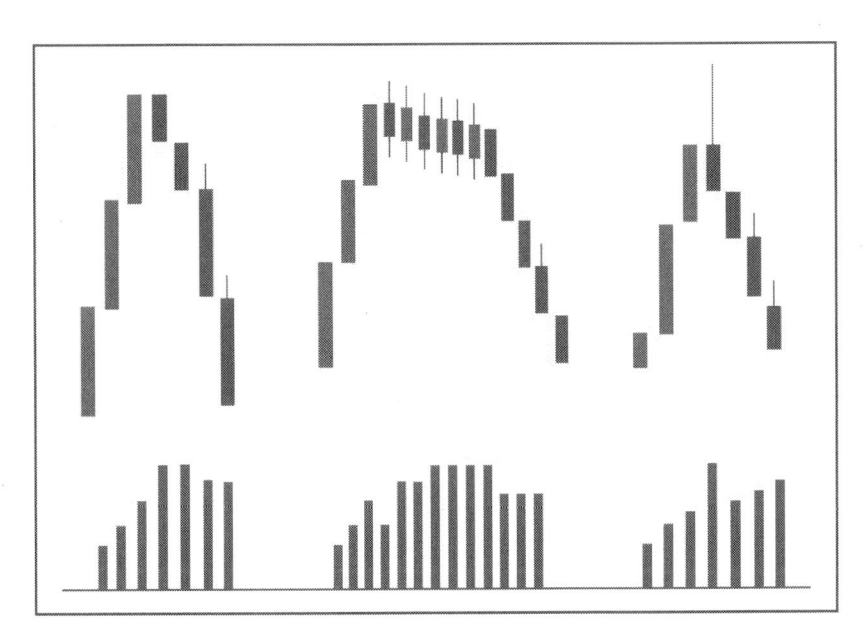

Visualization of bearish turn with great volume

The psychology behind the preliminary stop

We are now going to study the crossing of orders that occurs during such action. Remember, for someone to buy, there must be someone to sell.

Ask yourself what both the misinformed operator or "weak hand" and the well-informed operator or "strong hand" are doing at that point.

As we have commented, after determining that the market has reached a value price on which to start a campaign, the one that will be absorbing all the stock will be the big operator; and it is the ill-informed operators who are providing them with all the liquidity they need to build their positions.

We found different profiles of ill-informed operators that facilitate this fact:

- **The greedy**. There will be a group who see price move abruptly and enter the market to avoid being left out of a potential move in their favor.
- **The fearful**. This group has been holding losing positions for a long period of time and its limit is very close. After seeing the price move again against them and for fear of further increasing the loss, they finally decide to abandon their position.
- **The smart ones**. They will have been able to anticipate the turn and they will already be in the market; but their timing has not been precise and this movement takes them out making them jump their protection stops.

Uses of the preliminary stop

But then, what's the point of identifying this first stop event? As we have already mentioned, this is the first stop action of the previous trend movement and therefore we can draw two clear conclusions:

- Stop thinking about continuing to trade in favor of the previous trend at least initially, as the structure has yet to be confirmed as continuing or turning.
- This is an excellent point to take profits.

Preliminary Support

As we know that a bearish trend does not stop at once, it is possible to find numerous attempts to stop the fall before the successful one takes place. It's the inertia of the trend. It is like a moving vehicle; once the cruising speed is reached, even releasing the foot of the accelerator, the car will continue in the direction for a time by its own inertia.

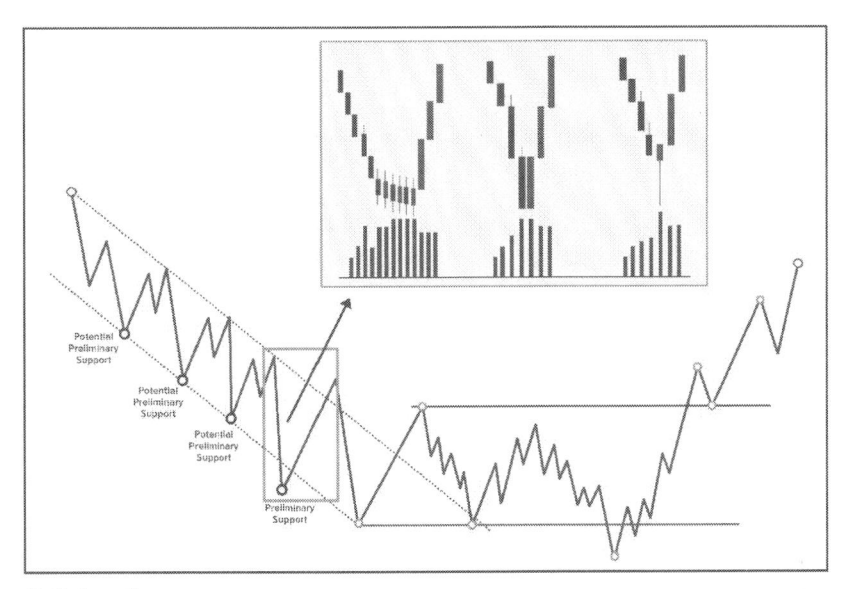

Preliminary Support

All those stop attempts are Preliminary Support. The more there are, the more likely it is that the last extreme of the bearish trend will finally occur without a significant increase in volume.

The fact of seeing repeated Preliminary Support suggests that the professional has been eliminating offer from the market and when the last minimum is reached, few will be willing to sell; and this will make that last extreme occur without a peak in volume. It will also be a Selling Climax, in this case without an ultra-high volume: the movement stops due to exhaustion. We'll talk about it when we develop this climate event.

Actually, they are Preliminary Support from a functional point of view; because for the Wyckoff methodology, the Preliminary Support as such will be the penultimate attempt to stop the downtrend (the last will be the Selling Climax). Therefore, it would be best to label them as potential Preliminary Support.

This potential PS will be confirmed as the genuine PS when the price develops the four Phase A events that establish the character change.

This first participation of the professional does not imply that the price should be rotated immediately. As we have already commented; in certain market conditions the price will develop a V turn accumulating all the necessary stock during the fall. We repeat that although this type of hypodermic accumulation is not the most likely, we must be alert to its possible development.

Preliminary Supply

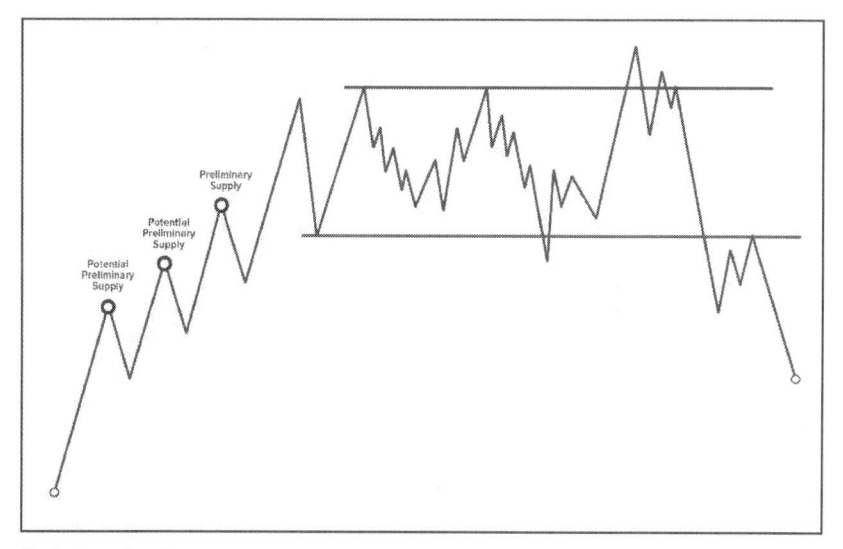

Preliminary Supply

Before the real Preliminary Supply takes place, the most logical thing would be to find ourselves with numerous previous attempts. These attempts should be labeled as potential Preliminary Supply.

The fact of seeing repeated Preliminary Supply suggests that the professional has been eliminating demand from the market and when the last maximum is reached, there will be few who are willing to buy; and this could cause that last extreme to occur without a significant volume.

Chapter 15 - Event #2: Climax

It is the second event of the methodology and appears after the stop attempt in the Preliminary Support/Supply.

In the accumulation examples we will call it Selling Climax (SC) while for the distributive structures we will label it Buying Climax (BC).

After the appearance of a large volume after a prolonged trend (potential standstill), we will be attentive to the possible identification of this climatic event. As we always say, this is one of the greatest benefits of the Wyckoff methodology: it provides us with a market context. We know what to look for.

But something important to keep in mind is that Preliminary Support/Supply events do not always appear within the sequence and their function can be performed at the same time by the climax event. That is why we insist time and again on the importance of giving the market some flexibility. We have a context and a basic sequence but it is necessary to allow the market to express itself freely, without trying to force it into our map, because wanting to exercise control over the market would be a mistake. The key to determine if we are directly before the climax will be obtained from the price; it will be necessary to see a strong reaction (Event No. 3) and a test (Event No. 4) that give the end of Phase A stopping the trend.

Keys to climax

Two things can happen after the climatic event; a reaction (Automatic Rally/Reaction) or a lateral movement. If a reaction appears, it will be followed by a Secondary Test; conversely, if a lateral movement takes place, the market will most likely continue in the direction of the previous trend.

A very relevant aspect is that this event needs to be tested to verify its authenticity (with the Secondary Test). A much lower volume in a subsequent test shows a decrease in selling pressure.

This event is known as "No Supply" and "No Demand" within the VSA (Volume Spread Analysis) approach.

Something very important to emphasize is that the climax will not necessarily be the greatest end of the structure. During the development of the same we could observe several tests (failed attempts to make minimums lower or maximums higher) during Phase B as well as the test event in Phase C (Spring/UTAD) that normally shakes the end of it.

How the climax appears on the graph

Although the principle does not change; it can manifest itself in different ways in terms of price and volume representation.

There is a prevailing belief within the world of price and volume analysis that this event should be viewed as a bar with increasing volume and expanding ranges. Even if this definition were correct, it would be incomplete because there are other forms of representation.

On the one hand, it can be seen on a set of bars with a relatively narrower range and with a high and constant volume during all of them. Another way would be on a single bar with high volume and a large wick at the bottom.

All these representations in the end denote the same thing: strong entry of buyer interest on the part of the large operators.

Regardless of the characteristics of the climatic event, when we look at the genuine Automatic Rally/Reaction and Secondary Test, we will automatically label the previous movement as Climax.

The psychology behind the climax

If we remember, due to the very nature of markets; for someone to be able to sell, someone else must have been willing to buy. So, it is a good idea to ask ourselves now, for example, who will be assuming all the sales that take place in the Selling Climax or the purchase of the Buying Climax.

Logic leads us to think that who is providing the counterparty is the big operator because it is he who has the ability to move the market and stop an abrupt fall or rise in price.

He has probably determined that the price is in an overextended condition and is happy to start a campaign in this area to absorb stock.

What are the reasons that lead the ill-informed operator to provide the liquidity that large operators need? We recall the origin of those liquidity providers already seen in the preliminary stop event:

- **The greedy**. There will be a group who see the climate movement and enter the market for fear of losing it.
- **The fearful**. Another group, generally with medium- to long-term positions, will have stockpiled and will have withstood much of the previous trend movement. They are in losses and when they see a new movement against them they decide to close their positions to avoid greater losses.
- **The smart ones**. A last group of traders, believing themselves to be the smartest in the class, will want to anticipate the turn and at that point they will probably already find themselves with open positions. This third type of counterparty occurs when the protection stop of these positions is skipped.

Uses of Climax

The identification of this event is very important because it signals the entry of professionals and therefore it is a supported action and quality.

What advantage can we gain by correctly identifying this event? As it is a stop action of the previous trend movement and pointing out the professional participation we can draw two clear conclusions:

- We must stop thinking about continuing to trade in favor of the previous trend. At least until we confirm whether the structure is about rotation or continuity.
- We are facing the last clear opportunity to take profit from our open positions if we did not do so on the stop event.

It is not recommended to start positions at this point as the assumed risk would be too high. However, it is true that some of the most experienced Wyckoff traders take advantage of this type of context to take short distance trades looking for the rebound to event #3 (Automatic Rally/Reaction).

Selling Climax

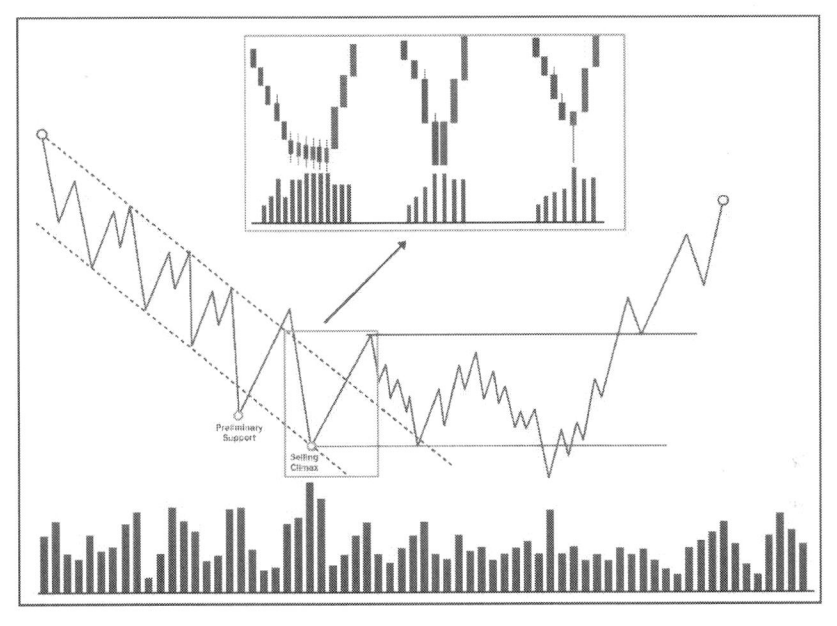

Selling Climax

This Selling Climax event is in the background similar to the Preliminary Support event. Both the way it can appear on the graph and the psychology behind the action are exactly the same. Also, we must treat it as Selling Climax potential since the confirmation will arrive to us when the two later events appear that confirm the end of the Phase A (Automatic Rally and Secondary Test).

The Selling Climax is a very powerful sign of strength. After a period of falling prices, you will reach a point where, supported by very negative news, the market will plummet rapidly. At that point, prices are now attractive for smart money and will begin to buy or accumulate at those low levels.

Selling Climax occurs after a significant downward movement. This is the second event to appear after the Preliminary Support and takes place within the Phase A stop of the previous bearish trend.

This climatic movement is generated by three reasons that we will detail next and that together provoke a snowball effect for which the price does not stop falling.

Within the Wyckoff methodology it has special relevance since with its appearance we can begin to define the limits of the range; and it is that its minimum establishes the lowest end of the structure (support zone).

The Selling Climax of exhaustion

A downward trend will not always end with a climatic volume. There is another way to come to an end and it occurs when the sale that is controlling the condition of the market is gradually disappearing.

Sellers stop being interested in lower prices and close their positions (take profits). This lack of aggressiveness of the shorts would create a potential market ground for exhaustion.

Obviously, this disinterest will be represented on the chart with candles of normal or narrow range and average or even low volume.

The curious thing about this action is that, even if we are not facing a climatic event that precedes the end of a trend, within the labeling of the structure we would continue to identify that minimum as the Selling Climax.

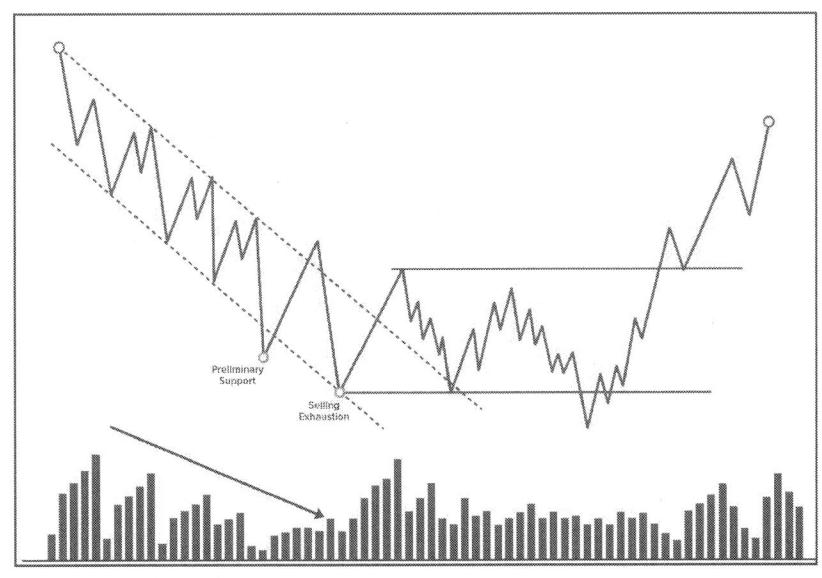

Selling Exhaustion

It must be made clear that the methodology originally did not treat this action as such Selling Climax; and it makes perfect sense because at no time did we observe this characteristic climax.

Although we always advocate treating market actions from a functional point of view, on this occasion we must observe this exhaustion from an analytical point of view in order to frame it within the structure's etiquette.

Perhaps we could propose to the whole Wyckoffian community a new event that would identify this end of the downward trend due to exhaustion. Something like "Selling Exhaustion" could be representative of the action you are referring to.

To emphasize of the Selling Exhaustion is that a signal of its possible appearance we obtain it when the price develops continuous actions of Preliminary Support every time lower.

Climatic actions will be observed as the downward movement develops where the overall volume is likely to decrease. This suggests that there is an absorption of sales where professionals have stopped selling aggressively and begin to take advantage of the bearish continuation to take profits from their shorts.

This can cause that market floor to develop without seeing above the last minimum an expansion in price ranges and volume. We will be before the new Selling Exhaustion.

Buying Climax

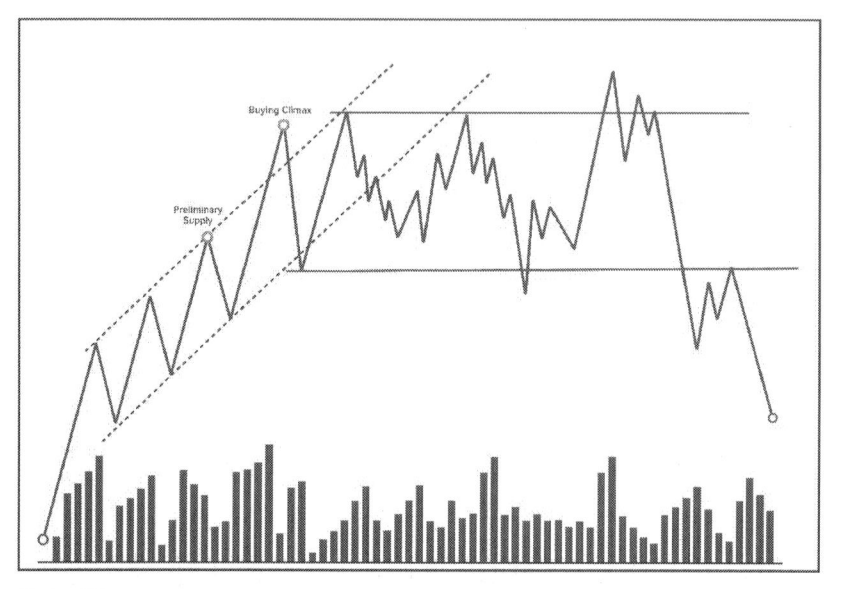

Buying Climax

Buying Climax is a powerful sign of market weakness. After an uptrend, the price, guided by favorable news and a buying irrationality on the part of the participants (ill-informed) will cause a rapid rise.

At this point, the market will have reached an uninteresting level to stay within, and well-informed traders will abandon their buying positions and even begin to position themselves short expecting lower prices.

The Buying Climax is the second event that appears after the Preliminary Supply and takes place within the Phase A stop of the previous bullish trend.

This climatic movement is originated by professional operators capable of initiating a price shift; and is followed by ill-informed operators who make their operational decisions generally on the basis of their emotions.

It's a trap. A deception where it seems that one is buying with a certain aggressiveness when in reality the intention behind it is totally the opposite. All purchases are being blocked with sales orders. The price cannot go up because someone with the ability to do so is absorbing all that stock.

With the appearance of the Buying Climax we begin to define the limits of the range; and it is that its maximum establishes the upper end of the structure (zone of resistance).

The similarities between Preliminary Supply and Buying Climax are total. Both the way it can appear on the graph and the psychology behind the action is exactly the same. The only difference between the two events is that Preliminary Supply fails to stop the previous uptrend, while Buying Climax does (at least temporarily).

Initially we must treat the Buying Climax as potential, since the confirmation will come to us when the two subsequent events appear confirming the end of Phase A (Automatic Reaction and Secondary Test).

The Buying Climax of exhaustion

An upward trend will not always end with a climatic volume. There is another way to come to an end and it occurs when the purchase that is controlling the condition of the market is gradually disappearing.

Buyers stop being interested in higher prices and close their positions (take profits). This lack of aggressiveness of the lengths would create a potential market ceiling due to exhaustion.

Obviously, this disinterest will be represented on the chart with candles of normal or narrow range and average or even low volume.

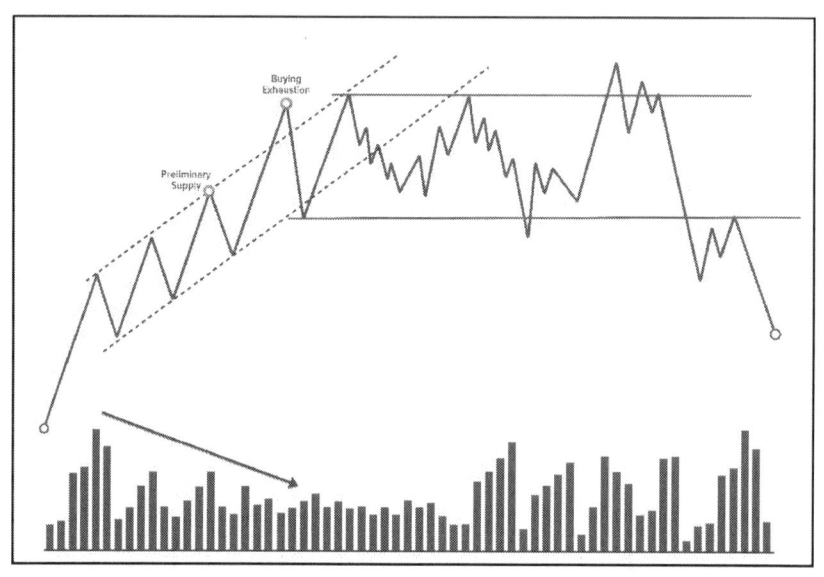

Buying Exhaustion

Although this action does not have the common characteristics of climatic events, within the methodology it is still labelled in the same way. That is why it would be interesting to differentiate between a climax stop and an exhaustion stop.

The proposal that is launched to the Wyckoffian community is the creation of a new event that serves to identify this end of the upward trend due to exhaustion. In this case, "Buying Exhaustion" seems to us to be the most suitable label.

One sign that we are possibly going to identify a Buying Exhaustion is the appearance of continuous higher and higher Preliminary Supply actions.

Preliminary Supply potentials will be observed where overall volume is likely to decrease. This suggests that there is a gradual absorption of purchases where professionals have stopped buying aggressively and begin to take advantage of the bullish continuation to take profits from their lengths.

This can cause that market ceiling to develop without seeing above the last maximum an expansion in price ranges and volume. We'll be looking at the new Buying Exhaustion.

Chapter 16 - Event #3: Reaction

After the appearance of the potential climax, there will be an automatic reaction that will visually leave a large movement in the opposite direction, thus confirming the climatic event.

This movement will be the most important since the market began the previous trend Phase. It suggests an aggressive entry of operators in the opposite direction and indicates a change of character.

This ChoCh (Change of Character) has great implications and is that it signals a change in the context of the market; the ChoCh appears to put an end to the previous trend and start an environment of lateralization in the price.

This change in behaviour must be confirmed with the last event of Phase A: The Secondary Test. With its appearance, we can confirm the new environment in which the market will move from that moment on.

The implications of its development

The distance travelled by this movement will be one of the elements we will consider later on as the structure develops in order to try to determine what the great professional is doing.

We must bear in mind that a short-distance reaction does not have the same implications as a significantly (in comparative terms) larger one.

For example, in a market where the latest upward movements have developed with an average of 50 points; and suddenly you see an Automatic Rally of 100 points, it suggests a stronger bottom.

It will be one of the elements that we will consider later on as the structure develops in order to try to determine what the great professional is doing.

When we see a movement that is intertwined, does not travel a great distance and without the appearance of a high volume, denotes that there is no great intentionality to push prices that way and suggests to us that the market is not yet in a state of equilibrium. Very possibly the later Secondary Test will be developed relatively soon and may go beyond the limits of the structure, denoting this imbalance.

If we observe this behaviour in a potential accumulation structure, we have to doubt that what is really taking place in the market is an accumulation for a later price increase. With this apparent weakness, it will be more sensible to think of a process of redistribution that leads to lower prices.

The same is true for analyses that denote a greater probability of distribution. If we see that the downward movement (AR in distribution) is intertwined, that it does not travel a great distance, that we have not seen a volume peak and that in addition the Secondary Test ends above the maximum established by the Buying Climax, we suspect that what is happening is a reaccumulation structure.

The anatomy of the reaction

Generally, the volume at the beginning of the movement will be large, we are at the end of the climatic event and it is normal that this price shift is made with a climatic volume (except for the appearance of Selling/Buying Exhaustion). As the movement progresses, the volume will decrease until it is relatively low in the end. This drying of the volume suggests a lack of interest in continuing to rise and will put an end to the Automatic Rally/Reaction.

With price ranges practically the same thing happens. At the beginning of the movement we will observe wide ranges, good candles/trend bars that will progressively narrow as they approach the end of the event.

Through continued practice you will develop the judgment necessary to know when the narrowing of ranges and the decrease in volume have reached a point at which movement is likely to stop. There are no fixed or mechanical rules, it's more a matter of judgment.

Reaction Uses

Delimits the limits of the structure. Within the structures of the Wyckoff methodology, it is one of the important elements since its end serves to identify one of the limits of the structure.

- The Automatic Rally establishes the upper limit of the range, delimiting a clear zone of resistance over which new sales are expected to appear in subsequent visits.
- The Automatic Reaction establishes the lower limit of the range, delimiting a clear support area over which new purchases are expected to appear in subsequent visits.

Identifies the climate event. The reaction is important as it will sometimes be unclear when the genuine climax has appeared. Therefore, on many occasions we recognize climate action after identifying the character change that follows this reaction.

- The Automatic Rally will identify the genuine Selling Climax.
- The Automatic Reaction will identify the genuine Buying Climax.

It provides us with the market context. After observing events 2 (Climax) and 3 (Reaction), we identify the change of character (ChoCh) of the market and we know that the price will test that climate action to develop the Secondary Test. We already have a market map. As we always say, this is very important because it provides us with an operational opportunity.

- If you have correctly identified the Selling Climax and now the Automatic Rally, you can download the timeframe to look for the development of a minor distribution structure that generates the end of Automatic Rally and the bearish turn that will look for the development of the Secondary Test.

- If you have identified the genuine Buying Climax and now the Automatic Reaction, you can download the timeframe to look for the development of a minor structure of accumulation that generates the end of Automatic Reaction and the bullish turn that will look for the development of the Secondary Test.

Opportunity to take benefits. If in an exercise of recklessness, you operated on the climatic event seeking precisely that rebound, this position should not be maintained throughout the development of the range, since in principle we cannot know whether it will be a structure of rotation or continuity. The most sensible thing would be to close the position on the Automatic Rally/Reaction obtaining the benefit of a Scalp.

Automatic Rally

The Automatic Rally is an upward movement of the price that develops after the end of the Selling Climax and that appears as the first signal of the buyer interest.

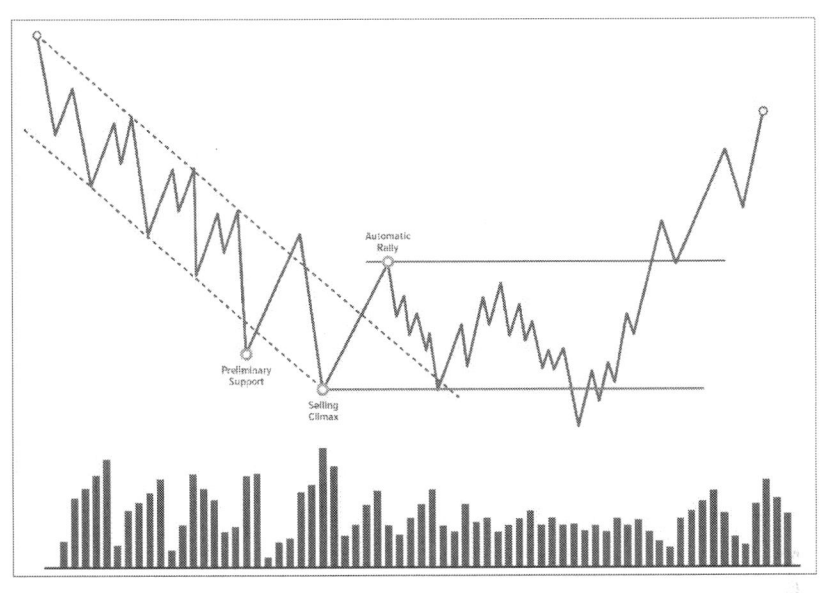

Automatic Rally

It is an event that is part of the Phase A stop of the previous trend and takes place after the Preliminary Support and the Selling Climax.

Why the Automatic Rally takes place

During the downward trend the price will have moved down a considerable distance and possibly reach a condition of overselling in the development of the Selling Climax where the following actions take place:

- **Exhaustion of the offer**. Aggressive sellers stop entering the market
- **Coverage of shorts**. Vendors who would have entered higher close their positions
- **Appearance of the lawsuit**. New buyers enter by observing the climate event

The market has reached uninteresting levels to continue selling, which will lead to a lack of supply. The withdrawal of sellers, both those who stop selling aggressively, as well as those who take profit from their shorts; together with the emergence of new buyers, who may have entered with reversal strategies to the average, will cause an easy push up prices.

The most normal thing is that buyers who have entered the Selling Climax do not intend to maintain their positions, since it is probably Scalp operations (short duration) and take profits during the Automatic Rally, putting an end to its development.

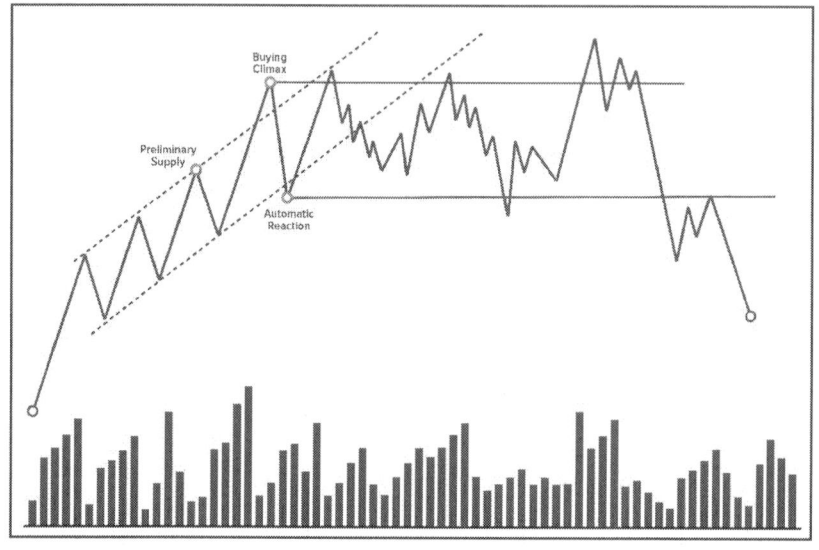

Automatic Reaction

Automatic Reaction

The Automatic Reaction is a significant downward price movement that appears as the first sign of selling interest. It is part of Phase A of the previous trend and develops after the Preliminary Supply and Buying Climax.

Why Automatic Reaction Occurs

The market will have moved upwards enough to produce a series of events that together give rise to the development of Automatic Reaction:

- **Exhaustion of demand**. There are no aggressive buyers willing to keep buying.
- **Length coverage**. Buyers who would have entered below close their positions by taking profits.
- **Appearance of the offer**. New vendors enter by observing the previous climatic event.

The previous market rally may have reached an overbought condition causing a lack of demand. This withdrawal of buyers, both those who stop buying aggressively, and those who take profit from their lengths; together with the emergence of new sellers will cause an easy push down prices.

Sellers who have entered the Buying Climax are surely speculating looking for a quick downward movement and will take profits during the Automatic Reaction, putting an end to its development.

Chapter 17 - Event #4: Test

Secondary Test

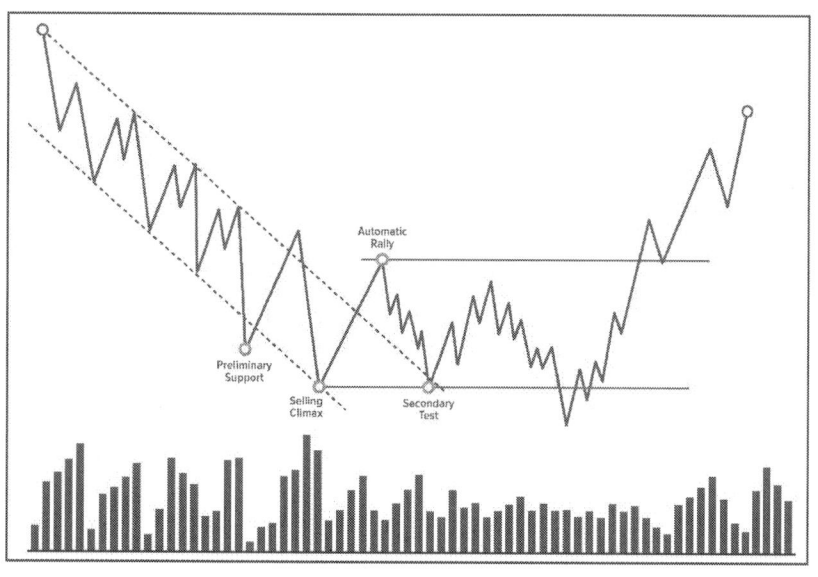

Secondary Test

The Secondary Test is the fourth event within the accumulation schemes of the Wyckoff methodology. Establishes the end of Phase A, stopping the previous trend, and gives rise to the beginning of Phase B, construction of the cause.

Functions of the Secondary Test

As with every event, one of the important points of its identification is that it identifies us with the context of the market; it gives us an indication of what to expect from now on. In this case, we went from being in a context of a downward trend to migrate to a context of lateralization in price.

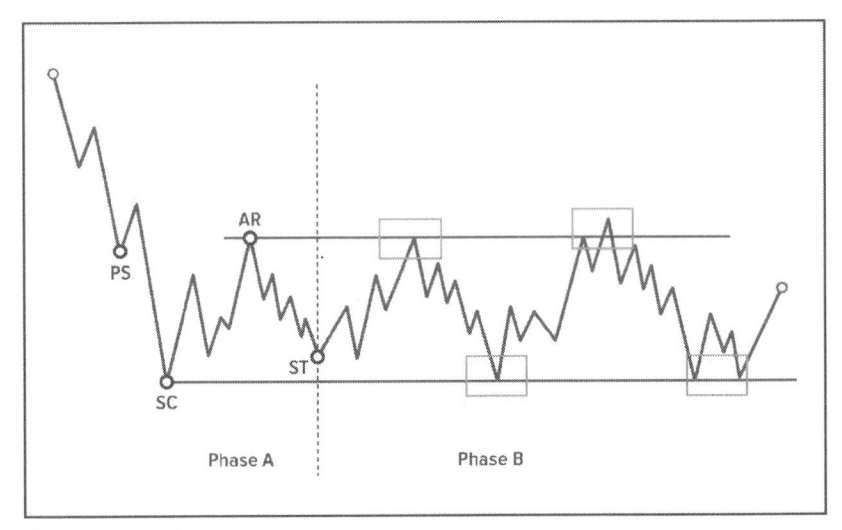

Trading in Phase B

This is very interesting since, as we know, the price behavior within Phase B will be a continuous fluctuation up and down between the limits of the structure.

With this background context, the type of trading that we will be able to develop here is to wait for the price at these extremes and look for a turn to the opposite side. Either directly from the time frame in which we are working with some configuration of candles, or reduce the time frame to look for a smaller structure of rotation there (if we are in the upper zone, we will look for a smaller structure of distribution, and if we are in the lower zone, we will look for a smaller structure of accumulation).

In functional terms, what the Secondary Test suggests to us is the confirmation of abandonment by aggressive sellers who have been pushing the price lower and lower during the development of the downward trend; to evolve into an equilibrium environment where buyers and sellers are comfortable negotiating (building the cause for the subsequent effect).

Secondary Test Features

For the Secondary Test to be successful, the bearish movement must be made with a narrowing in the price ranges and a smaller volume than that seen in the Selling Climax.

Although some authors defend the position that it is necessary for the Secondary Test to be kept above the minimum established by the Selling Climax, the truth is that it is a good moment to remember that the market is not a rigid entity, but that it is in constant change due to its own nature and that therefore it would be convenient to grant certain flexibility to the price movements.

With this in mind, we can attribute that a Secondary Test above the minimum Selling Climax would be seen with a neutral connotation when identifying which side (buyers and sellers) have more control of the market. So, it would be a good way to identify a certain imbalance on the part of buyers if the Secondary Test we see is performed over the upper half of the range; and it would likewise identify a certain imbalance in favor of sellers if the Secondary Test ends slightly below the Selling Climax.

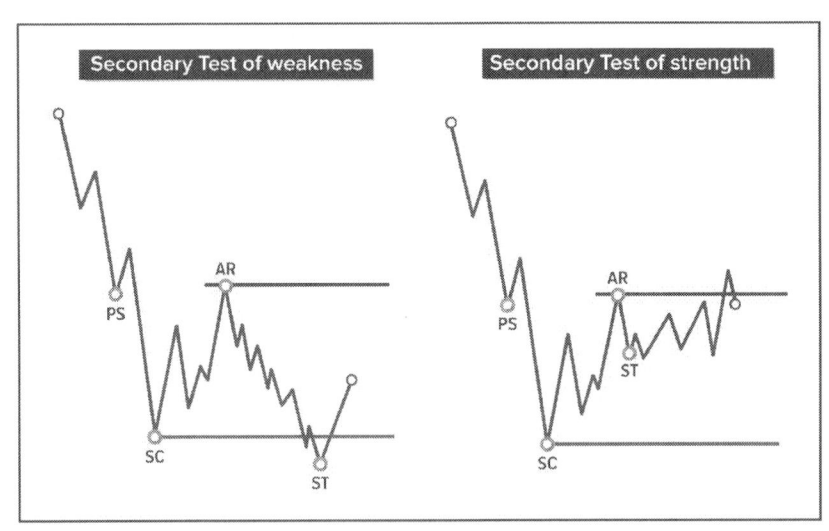

Types of Secondary Test

This characteristic, together with the rest of the elements that have been commented on, as well as those that will follow, is an indication to consider when assessing whether we are dealing with an accumulation or distributive structure. It is a question of putting the greater probability on our side and therefore, the more of these signs in favour of a direction, the greater strength our analysis will have.

The really important thing to look at is, in order of importance: the decrease in volume and the narrowing of the ranges. As we know, volume reflects activity and therefore, low activity after a climatic event denotes a lack of interest in that side.

The Secondary Tests of Phase B

Although the "official" Secondary Test is the one that appears in Phase A, it is a type of behaviour that we will continue to observe in different Phases of the development of the structure.

Once Phase B has begun, we are going to be awaiting any type of test on one of the two extremes of the range.

This type of test allows us to evaluate the strength and weakness of buyers and sellers. Occasionally, tests will even be performed at both the top and bottom ends of the structure.

Depending on the subsequent effect of the range (whether it is accumulation or distribution), the tab pages are differentiated for the same actions. As it is logical, until the price does not leave the range we cannot know what was the real intention behind the cause that was being constructed and therefore, in real time any labelling should be valid.

Beyond seeing the market in a conventional way, we will also think in terms of functionality and differentiate price behaviors from two points of view: as a concept (action) and as an event (depending on the location).

Secondary Test on the upper end

The price passes through the previous maximum created in the stop action but does not move too far away before re-entering the range, leaving a slight Shake.

Initially it is a movement that denotes background strength as the price has been able to penetrate the resistance zone of the range; and this could not happen if there were no aggressive buyers present.

A subsequent evaluation will confirm whether it is really a strength test in which stock has been absorbed (bought, accumulated) with the intention of increasing; or whether it is a share on which it has been distributed (sold) with the aim of bringing the price down.

This new maximum can be used to establish a new upper end on which to look for effective bullish rupture (in Phase D) or bearish shaking of the structure (in Phase C).

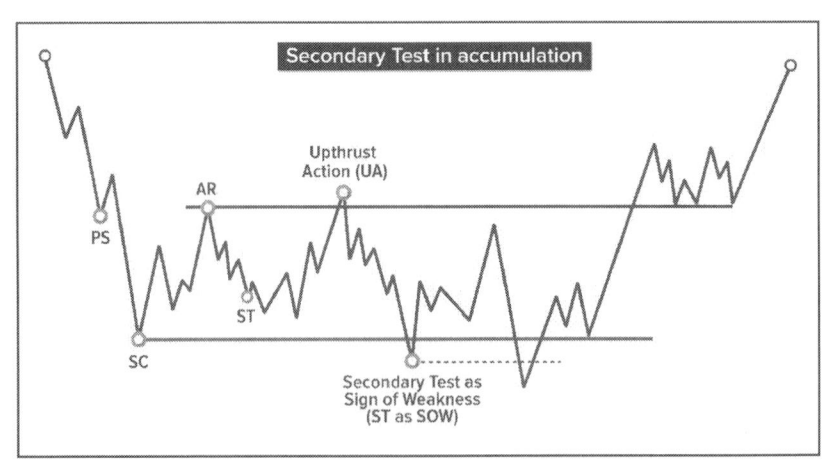

Secondary test in accumulation

When the range is accumulation/accumulation, this event will be labeled as **Upthrust Action (UA)**; while if it is a distribution or redistribution structure we will label it as **Upthrust (UT)**.

This is the only difference between these tags; if we believe with the clues that we have until now that the probability is in an accumulation range we will label it as Upthrust Action; and if we believe that there is more probability that it is being distributed we will label it as Upthrust.

When the UA occurs and the price remains above resistance for some time before falling, this behavior can be labeled as **minor Sign of Strength (mSOS)**. It would be a kind of test that denotes greater strength.

Secondary Test on the lower end

It's a minimal structure test that produces a lower minimum. It is due either to the aggressiveness of the sellers or a lack of interest of the buyers, which suggests that it is likely new tests to that area in the future.

This type of test denotes a lot of fundamental weakness. Well-informed traders know that the price is overvalued and they have an urgency to sell. Hence the extreme weakness.

From this new minimum, we can draw another level of support on which to wait for the effective bearish break or the final jerk before the upward trend movement.

If we are dealing with an accumulation structure, we will label this event as **Secondary Test as Sign of Weakness (ST as SOW)**. There is generally a better chance that this event will occur when the Secondary Test of Phase A has produced a lower minimum. There is an extreme weakness in the market and this area will need to be tested in the future.

When the range is distribution or redistribution we label this event as minor Sign of Weakness (mSOW). One indication that we may be facing a mSOW is whether the Secondary Test of Phase A is a poor bullish movement, with very little path (lack of buyer interest).

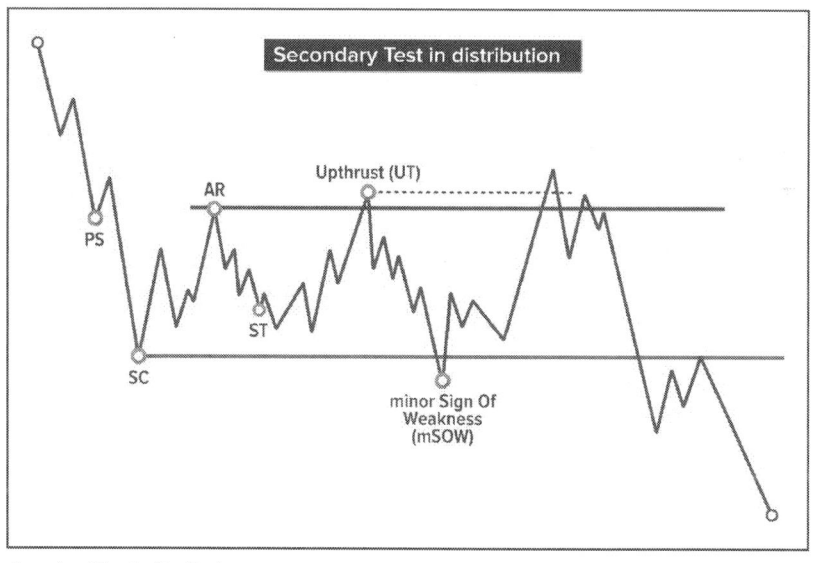

Secondary Test in distribution

As we say, we can only know which labeling is correct once the range has been confirmed in one direction or the other. Therefore, in order not to complicate it more than necessary, a simple solution could be to label such events as **Secondary Test in Phase B (ST in B)**, a label that you will also find in some analysis of the methodology.

The generic test

A test, by definition, is an attempt, evaluation or examination of something. In the case of Volume Spread Analysis (VSA), it is a test to confirm who has control of the market.

If professional traders have higher interests, they will want to make sure that the bid has been eliminated or absorbed before starting the upward movement. Conversely, if they foresee lower prices, they will do their best to confirm that there are no buyers willing to complicate their downward movement.

As the market enters an area where previously there was a high volume two things can happen:

- That the volume is now low, which clearly indicates lack of interest and suggests that the market is now prepared for a trend movement in favour of less resistance. Valid test.
- That the volume is still high (relatively), which would indicate that there are still operators willing to keep pushing the price. Test not valid. The optimum here would be to wait either for repeated tests to appear until it can be confirmed that there is no stock left available; or that the market continues in favour of its last movement.

Due to the above, tests can be a great time to enter the market, because if the test is valid, we will be "betting" in favor of the force that presses more and that in theory has greater control of the market.

Where to look for tests

Due to its generic nature, it is an action that can be useful to make trading and investment decisions in different market contexts, being the most recommendable:

Test after shock

Known as the Spring test or the Upthrust test, it takes place during Phase C of the test, prior to the rupture of the structure.

This is the moment in the market when we can have the best risk/benefit ratio; since if the test is genuine, we will be very close to the end of the structure (where the Stop Loss order should be placed) and the route to the Creek could be quite wide (to take as first Take Profit or management).

Test after breakout

It takes place during Phase D, where the price has started the trend movement within the range and this is a critical moment as what is being evaluated is whether the Creek break will be valid or whether it will be a shake.

The risk/benefit ratio is not as generous as the one we may have in the test after shock, but even so we may have a great opportunity because if we are right in the analysis, the price will develop the effect of all the cause that has been built during the development of the range.

An example of Stop Loss location in this case could be to place it in the middle part of the structure, assuming that if the price reaches that level, more than an effective break we could be before a shake.

At the Take Profit level, you can use technical tools such as Fibonacci projections, a simple 1:1 projection of the total distance of the structure; or better yet, place it in some area where there is expected to be liquidity waiting.

Trend test

It should be noted that the price is in Phase E of the structure where the market begins to move tendentially out of range.

If the trend is very fast, it will sometimes take time to stop at least temporarily to develop a new scheme in favor of that trend. For such cases of speed, we can seek to develop this action, which will give us an opportunity to join the movement.

If the technical objectives of the structure have already been covered, I would particularly quarantine the entry. In the case of Stop Loss, I would expect the development of a Shake + test out of range to place the order at its end. For the Take Profit, the best thing to do is to keep looking for areas of liquidity as we know that it is very likely that the price will go in your search.

How the Test appears on the graph

In Volume Spread Analysis these types of candles are known as No Demand and No Supply.

The test is considered valid when the candle has a volume lower than that of the two previous sails, denoting as we say that lack of interest in that direction.

When we are faced with an environment of possible background strength (such as a Spring, a Creek bullish break or an uptrend) we will look for the test, in addition to showing a smaller volume than that of the previous two candles, to be produced on a bearish (No Supply) candle. The smaller the range of the candle, the better.

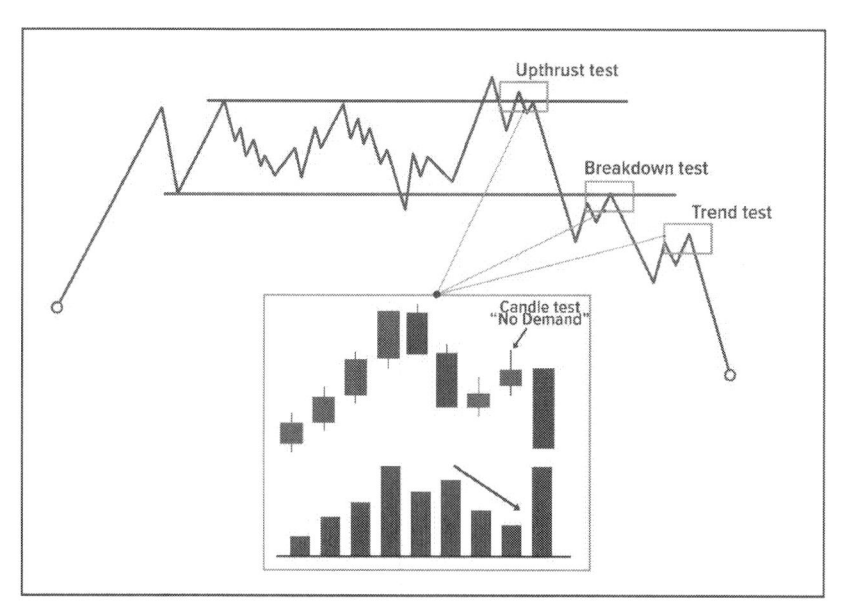

Tests on Shorts Positions

On the contrary, when our analysis tells us that we are possibly facing a weak market environment (such as an Upthrust, a bearish break in the Creek or in the middle of a bearish trend), we will look for the test to take place on a narrow range bull candle (No Demand).

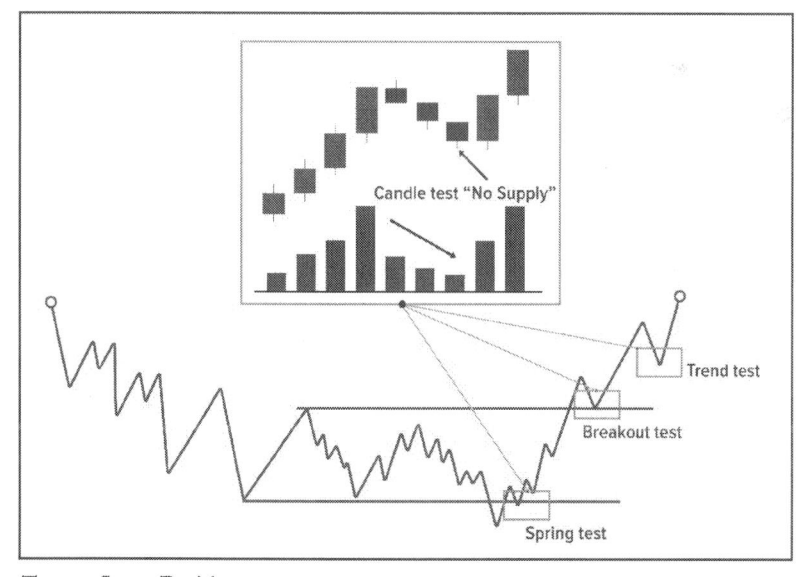

Test on Long Positions

The difference between the Secondary Test and the Generic Test

Conceptually it is the same action: movement that develops to evaluate the commitment of operators in one direction and that must necessarily appear with a decrease in the price ranges and volume to take it as valid.

The only difference is that the Secondary Test is a specific event of the Wyckoff methodology, with the connotations at a structural level already commented; and the generic test is a global event, well known in the VSA methodology (Volume Spread Analysis) that focuses primarily on the action itself and what its result suggests to us.

Chapter 18 - Event #5: Shaking

Shaking is the key event all Wyckoff operators are waiting for. There is no other event that adds greater strength to the analysis and this makes it, from my point of view, the most important event that can occur in the financial markets.

After a period in which large traders will have built up a large part of the position they want, they use this behaviour as a turning point when it comes to creating the trend movement that will take the price out of range.

In order for us to be waiting to see a potential shake, two actions must have occurred previously:

- The stop of the previous trend movement, whether with climatic volume or not.
- The construction of a significant cause. This is the development of Phase B, in which we deduce that the professional has been absorbing stock.

Addition game 0

As we know, due to the functioning of the financial markets based on the law of supply and demand, in order for an order to be executed, it must be paired with another order whose intention is the opposite. This means that for a sale (bid) transaction to be executed, it must be matched with a purchase (ask) transaction and vice versa.

This is very important to know since in the event we are dealing with, as in the other two cheating events (Preliminary Stop and Climax) all orders whose origin comes from ill-informed operators or weak hands are being absorbed by well-informed operators or strong hands.

The critical factor when analyzing this event is to determine the aggressiveness with which the key zone is being broken and how the market reacts immediately afterwards to this action.

Behavior

The action is simple: it is a movement of rupture of a previous liquidity area (areas where there will be located a large number of pending orders of execution) that initially denotes intentionality towards the direction of the rupture but that in reality is a new deception.

What will happen is a false break where the big traders will assume all those pending orders in order to start the trend movement they expect.

This is the way financial markets move: by the search for liquidity. If large traders were not able to find the counterparty they need to match their orders, the market would be impossible to move. Therefore, they need to create the feeling that this is a genuine break movement in order to attract more traders and absorb all those orders.

If we take any graph, independently of the market or temporality, we will see that for any significant trend movement, a Shake has previously developed. It's necessary. That crossing of orders is the gasoline they need to get around.

Understanding this will elevate your trading some levels because you will begin to be more aware of this possibility and over time you will learn to profit from its behavior.

How the Spring appears on the graph

Normally, shaking will come in different forms:

On 1 candle

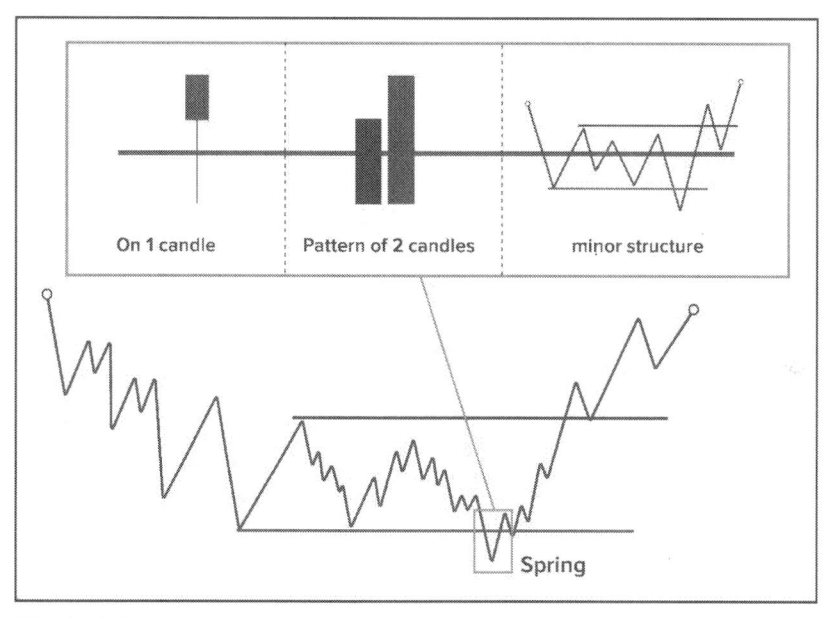

How the shake appears on the graph

This is the commonly known hammer sail. It is a candle that penetrates the zone of liquidity and that returns practically the totality of the movement inside that same candle, leaving a significant tail in its end.

These fuses what denotes is a rejection of prices to keep moving in that direction. Aggressiveness has been found on the part of the operators that were waiting in the opposite direction to the breakout and these have managed to capture at least temporarily with the control of the market.

Pattern of 2 or more candles

The background of the action is exactly the same as for the example of a candle. The only difference is that on this possibility the behavior develops over a greater temporal space.

The fact that the price takes longer before reversing and recovering the previously established breakout zone is a symptom of less strength for the shock. In other words, the less time the turn occurs, the greater the strength will denote the shock.

Minor structure

In this possibility, the price is kept for a longer period of time in position of potential shake.

The control of the market is not very defined and that is why a smaller structure is required which will eventually act as a function of the Shake of the larger structure. This is a clear example of the importance of context.

- In potential Spring position, we are looking for a smaller accumulation structure that will generate the bullish turn.
- In potential position Uptrust After Distribution we are looking for a smaller distribution structure that will generate the bearish turn.

Shaking functions

This movement initiated by the big operators has several functions:

Expel rupture operators from the market

Previously we presented them as greedy. They are those operators who see the price make a new extreme and thinking that it is a break that will have continuity, enter the market by adding more pressure to prices.

It is important to note that it is not only manual operators who, guided by their emotions, will enter the market. An innumerable number of automatic strategies programmed to operate breakout systems will generate input signals at these levels.

These robots may activate other momentum strategies, which will add even more pressure to the movement, which is why these types of shocks are often identified with a considerable increase in volume. It is an important trading area for many strategies and will therefore lead to the crossing of a large number of orders.

Expelling the fearful from the market

This group has been holding losing positions for a long period of time and its limit is very close. After seeing the price move again against them and for fear of further increasing the loss, they finally decide to abandon their position.

Kick the smart ones out of the market

Generally, they tend to have a good market reading and have correctly anticipated the price turn, but have rushed into entry. They may have already sold on the climatic event or on some minor Spring within the range.

This new unexpected final shock for them makes them abandon their position by executing their protection stops.

Succeeding with the maneuver

The professionals who unbalance the market and cause the breakout movement, take advantage of the displacement caused by the rupture operations and close their positions obtaining a profit with the difference.

Indications to know if we are facing a potential shakeout

The two elements to observe in order to try to determine a greater probability that we are facing a shock instead of an effective break are the following:

<u>The type of ST that happens in Phase B</u>

If we have previously identified a Secondary Test in the form of Upthrust Action (UA), this denotes greater strength to the buyers and therefore in zone of minimum breakout of the structure we favor the Spring instead of the bearish breakout.

If what has left the price is a Secondary Test in the form of Sign of Weakness (mSOW), denotes strength of the sellers and in zone of maximum rupture of the structure we favor that happens the Upthrust instead of the effective bullish rupture.

<u>Price behaviour after breakout</u>

If after the breakout of the lower part of the structure the price fails to stay below and re-enters the range again, it denotes strong purchase entry and adds greater probability that the breakout is false and that a Spring is therefore developing.

If after the break in resistance the price fails to stay above the level, it denotes weakness and adds a greater probability that the break is false and therefore an upthrust will develop.

Avoid labeling errors

It is important to clarify that the Shake can only be labeled as Spring or Upthrust After Distribution when it originates the rupture movement of the structure.

Spring must necessarily cause the range to break up. Anything other than this should not be labeled as Spring. It will simply be a test.

The same goes for the Upthrust After Distribution. Anything other than this bullish jerk causing the subsequent bearish break of the structure should not be labeled UTAD. A UTAD is the shaking event of the maximums of the structure but it must also cause the bearish break and the beginning of the tendential movement out of range.

I repeat, to be faithful to the methodology, anything other than that would be badly labeled.

Spring/Shakeout

The term Spring is an abbreviation of the word "Springboard".

This concept was presented by Robert G. Evans, an outstanding student of Richard D. Wyckoff and is a refinement of the original concept developed by Wyckoff, which is known as Terminal Shakeout. Wyckoff referred to this term as a position that reaches the market during the development of an accumulation range in which the price is in a position to leave it to initiate an upward movement.

We recall that an accumulation range is a Phase of the market cycle (which is composed of the accumulation, uptrend, distribution and downtrend Phases) in which large market operators perceive value in the price (they find it undervalued) and carry out a buying process with the intention of selling at higher prices and making a profit from the difference.

The Spring event describes a bearish movement that breaks a previous support area and whose purpose is to carry out a transfer of shares from the weak hands (traders potentially manipulable due to their ignorance of the functioning of the market and because they operate based on their emotions) to the strong hands (large traders).

Types of Spring

At the moment of the breakout of the support, we must remain very attentive and carefully observe the behavior of the price and volume. If we are already within a buy position, depending on how the price drops we will decide whether to stay within the trade or exit immediately. If you see a strong rebound from the level with a slight increase in volume, it indicates that the value is developing technical strength.

Three types are differentiated on the basis of the degree of supply observed at the time of breakout:

Spring #1 or Terminal Shakeout

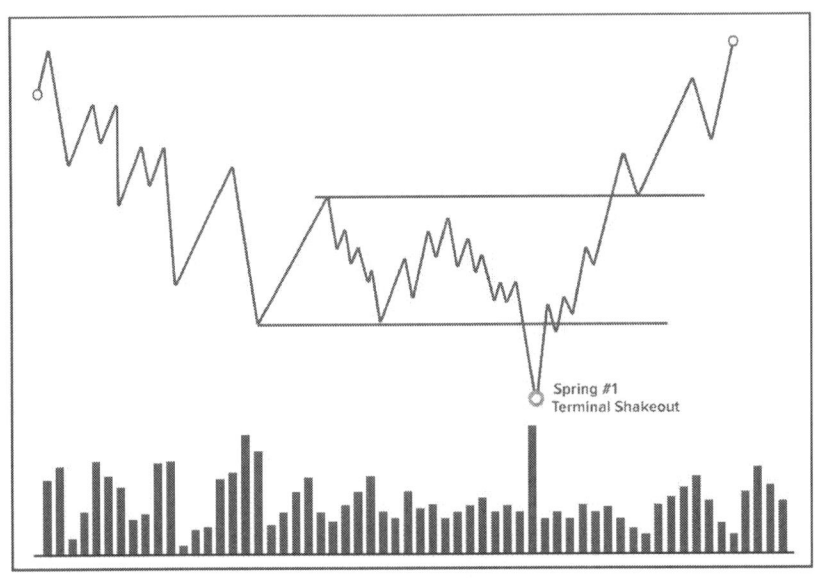

Spring #1 or Terminal Shakeout

The offer appears strongly (great seller interest). This is evidenced by a sudden increase in volume and an expansion of price ranges that produce a large penetration of the support line.

In essence, Spring and Terminal Shakeout are all about the same action: a bearish move that breaks through a previous support area. But there are differences between them, and these can be found in the intensity (volume) and scope of their development; while Spring is used to define shorter movements with a light or moderate volume; Terminal Shakeout is used to define movements with a much deeper penetration and with a high volume.

The offer is in control of the situation. There is extreme weakness and the price falls. For this type of Spring to be successful, there must be a strong inflow of demand that drives the price back up with wide price ranges and a relatively high volume.

A first indication that demand may be entering is if after penetration, the volume remains high but price ranges begin to decrease.

If demand does not appear, the price will continue to fall and you will have to build a new accumulation area before a substantial upward movement can take place.

Spring #2

Moderate penetration is observed as the price breaks down with an increase in both volume and price ranges.

There is a floating offer (operators willing to sell), but it is not as overwhelming as in Spring #1. That latent offer will have to be absorbed by the professionals in case they want to make rise to the price, reason why the most probable thing is that we will see successive tests to this zone.

Spring #2

Spring #3

There is an exhaustion of the offer (lack of aggressive saleswoman). This is evidenced by a slight reach in the break, with a decrease in volume and a narrowing of price ranges; suggesting a total lack of interest on the downside.

This is a very powerful Spring on which you can directly take purchase positions.

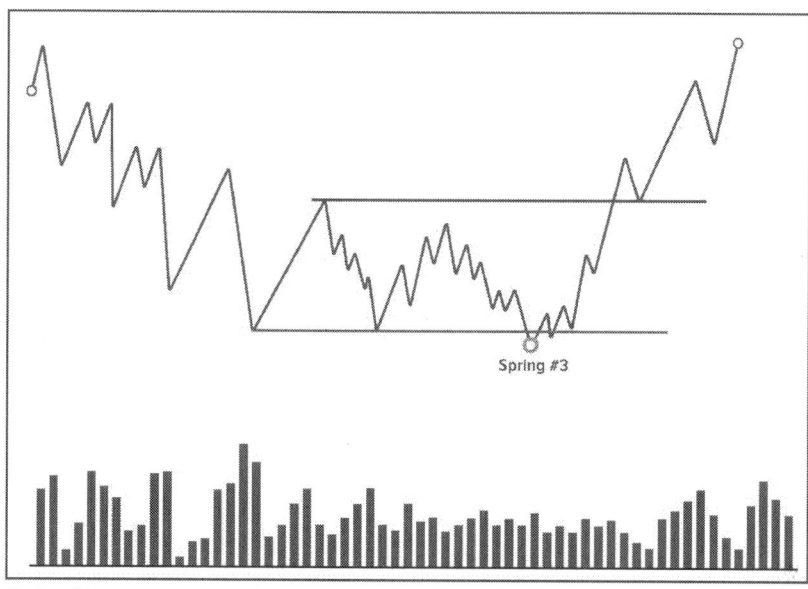

Spring #3

We can also find a last variant in which the event takes place within the limits of the range. This event denotes greater background strength, although professionals prefer the Shake to occur beyond the range because it does a better job of cleaning up the remaining supply of weak hands.

Spring action is an important sign of strength since failure to break provides us with a greater degree of confidence when it comes to acting at a later date.

The Ordinary Shakeout

Spring and Terminal Shakeout are two similar events which occur during the development of an accumulation range. But there is another variant; the Ordinary Shakeout, which is defined as a strong bearish push without extensive prior preparation that occurs during the development of an uptrend (reaccumulation). This is the main difference: the location.

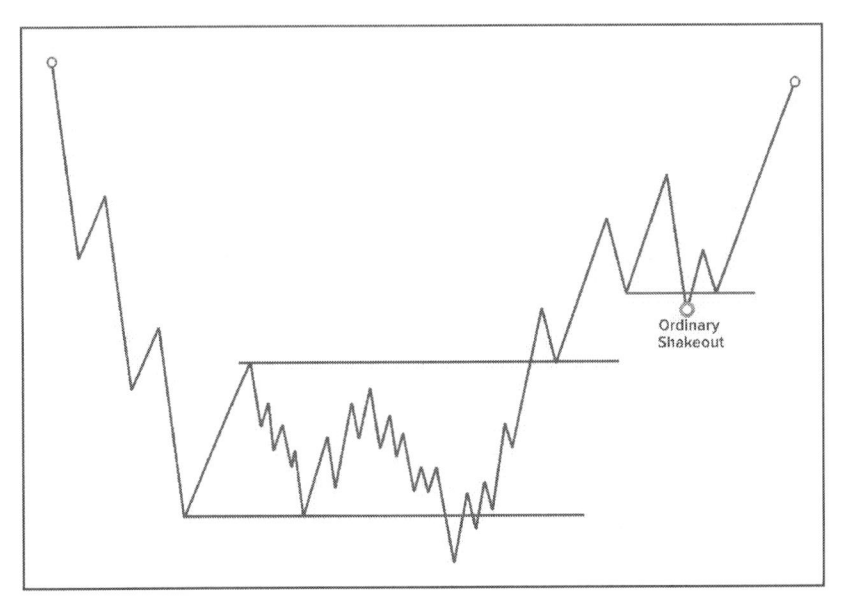

Ordinary Shakeout

The Ordinary Shakeout is characterized by wide price ranges and an increase in volume. However, the volume can be high, medium or low.

The Spring test

With the exception of Spring #3, in the other variants it is necessary for the event to be tested since the present offer has been observed and the positive result is not guaranteed.

Be very cautious if the testing process has not taken place as it may take place at a future time. For the test to be successful, it should be developed with a narrowing of the ranges, a decrease in volume and should be kept above the level of the Spring/Shakeout. All this would indicate an exhaustion of the offer and suggests that the price is ready to initiate the bullish movement with relative ease, representing a good buy signal.

If the test does not meet these characteristics, it is considered to be a poor-quality test and suggests further testing at a later date as a Spring with significant volume needs to be successfully tested before upward movement can begin.

We must train ourselves to anticipate the possible outcome of the event and be prepared to act on our behalf quickly and decisively.

UpThrust After Distribution (UTAD)

An Upthrust After Distribution is the bullish shock that occurs as a Phase C test event within the distribution and redistribution ranges.

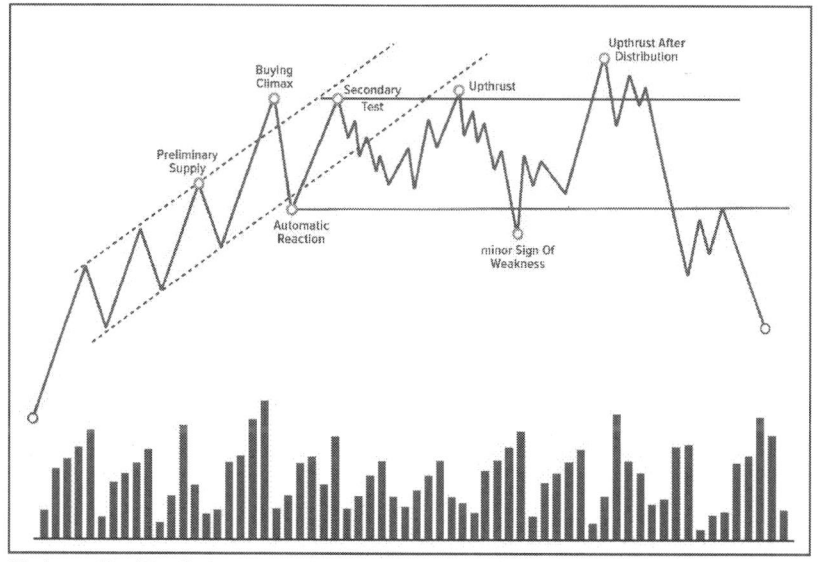

Upthrust After Distribution

This is an upward movement whose aim is to go test the ability of buyers to take prices higher to reach a key area, such as the break of previous highs.

Theoretically it is an Upthrust (UT), but when it happens in Phase C, it is called UTAD regardless of whether there were previous Upthrusts in Phase B because a previous distribution process has already taken place.

In this action, the volume that will be observed will be moderate or strong, evidencing the quantity of orders that will be crossing in this key zone.

The minor Upthrust After Distribution

As with the minor Spring, it is a bullish jerk that occurs within the structure.

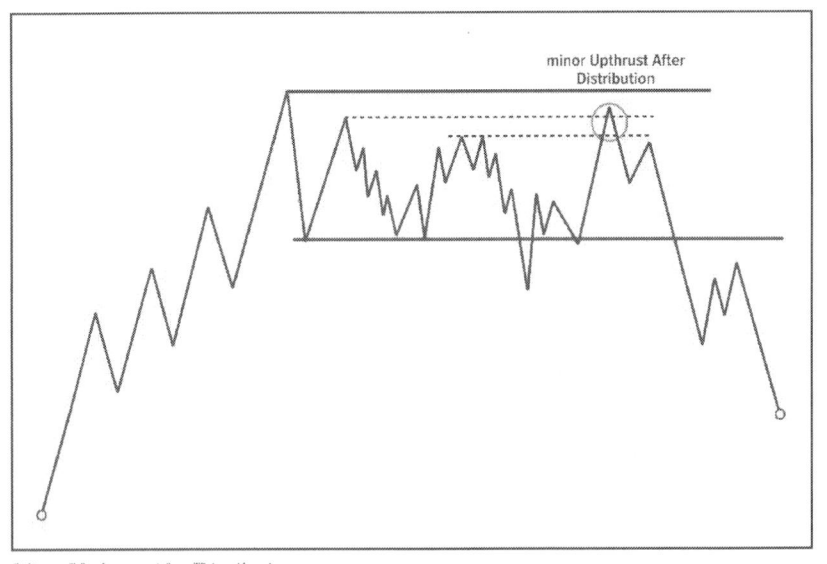

Minor Upthrust After Distribution

This Shake will reach some previous highs and although the ideal is to wait for the trap to occur at the total limits of the structure, in reality this type of minor Shake denotes greater control on the part of the sellers as they have not allowed the price to rise further and have appeared aggressively selling on those previous highs.

Although it is true that the UTAD is only the shaking event of the maximums of the structure, it is more interesting to think in functional terms and although this movement has not reached these total maximums, it is still a shaking at local maximums. This is why I consider it interesting to label this event as a minor UTAD as well, although the methodology may simply treat it as a Last Point of Supply (LPSY).

The Upthrust After Distribution Test

Although it can happen, a Secondary Test does not always appear after the UTAD. This is due to the large amount of supply entering the market, which causes the immediate bearish movement in the form of Sign of Weakness.

As with the Spring, it is generally better for the test to take place. The fact that the test does not appear may mean the loss of an opportunity, but waiting for it to happen will help you avoid taking a possible bad short position on an action that is actually a genuine bullish break (JAC/MSOS).

If there is a test, it should show less enthusiasm than the one seen about UTAD. This is generally reflected by a halt in movement below the UTAD level and a reduction in price and volume ranges, which indicates an exhaustion of buyers and confirms the distribution scenario. On the ceiling of this rise one can take sales positions.

If the test does not fall below the level that establishes the maximum UTAD or the volume is higher, you should doubt the shock even if the price is making lower maximums. The most sensible thing is to wait for some additional signal before selling (new shocks and successive successful tests).

Terminal Upthrust

It resembles Terminal Shakeout. It has the same features as a normal Upthrust but the scope of action is usually more severe. The volume may be extremely high or the penetration unusually large. Even so, the result is the same. In a short period of time the price re-enters the range, indicating strong downward pressure.

Ordinary Upthrust

Like the Ordinary Shakeout, it is a shakeout with little preparation during the development of the downward trend movement.

It is a very interesting opportunity to go into short since we would be operating in favor of the last distribution.

Chapter 19 - Event #6: Breakout

After the Phase C test event (shock or LPS), the price will develop a trend movement in the direction of the least resistance.

The great professionals have already absorbed all the stock they need for their positions and have verified (through the Shake and the test) that they will not find much resistance in the subsequent advance of the price in their favour.

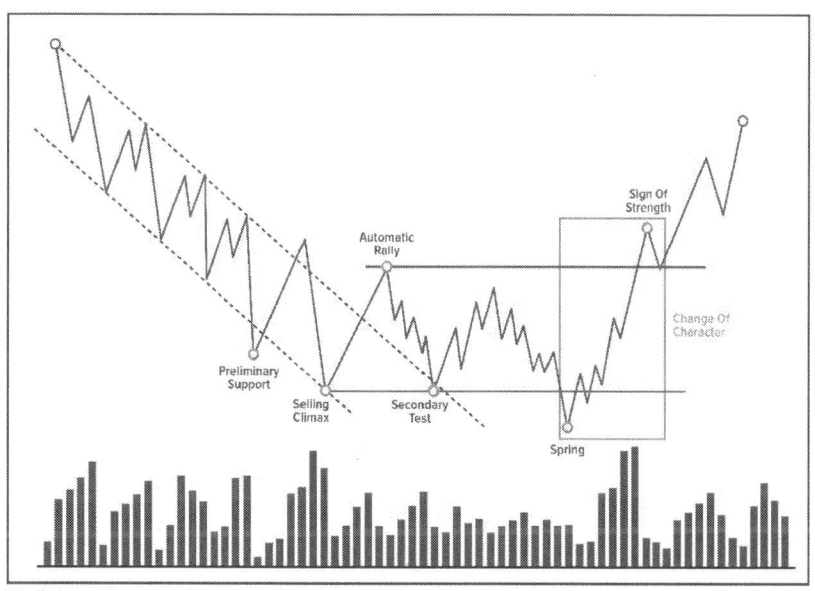

Bullish breakout and Change of Character

The market is in imbalance and this provokes a strong movement that breaks the structure initiating the development of the cause that has been constructed previously.

This breakout movement itself is not an opportunity to trade; it only alerts us to a possible opportunity in the very near future. This opportunity is found in the immediate action, in the confirmation test.

Change of Character
This is the second Change of Character (ChoCh) in the structure. We recall that the first occurs with Reaction Event #2, in which the market moves from a trend state to a range context.

In this occasion, this new ChoCh changes the context of the market putting an end to the lateralization of the price and giving beginning to a new trending Phase.

ChoCh is not only a strong movement; it is composed of two events: a strong movement and a slight retreat. This set forms the ChoCh. The change of character is identified from the origin of Phase C until the end of Phase D.

How it appears on the graph
We find ourselves in an environment of speed and this causes that movement to develop by means of candles in which a relative increase is observed in the ranges of the price as well as an increase in the volume.

This movement will fluidly break previous levels of liquidity denoting strong momentum. It is the representation of the market imbalance and the aggressiveness shown by traders.

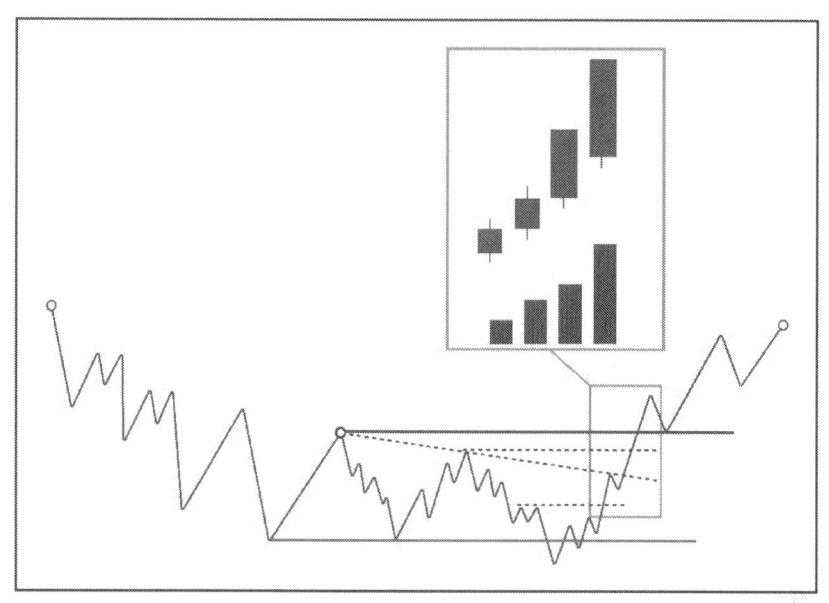

How the bullish breakout appears on the graph

The breakout without volume

Generally, ruptures should occur with increasing volume, although it is true that sometimes we could see such stocks without a particularly high volume increase. This suggests that the stock that remains available is essentially low and that therefore the operators in control will not need to make any special effort to easily displace the price.

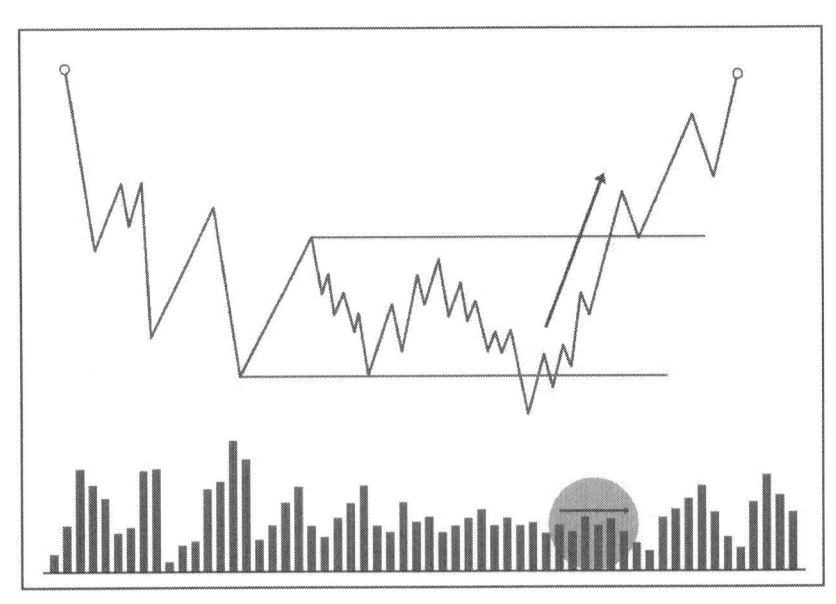

The breakout without volume

For the example of bullish breakout, if we see that it occurs with narrow range candles and a volume in the middle, in principle we should be wary of its intentionality; but what may happen is that there is very little floating supply, that is, there are very few traders willing to sell. So the absence of sellers coupled with moderate aggressiveness on the part of buyers can lead to such an upward rupture without relatively high volume.

Keys to the breakout event

It is a key moment since we could be facing a potential shaking event, so it is essential to make a judicious evaluation of the price action and the volume after the break. To do this, we can help ourselves with some clues:

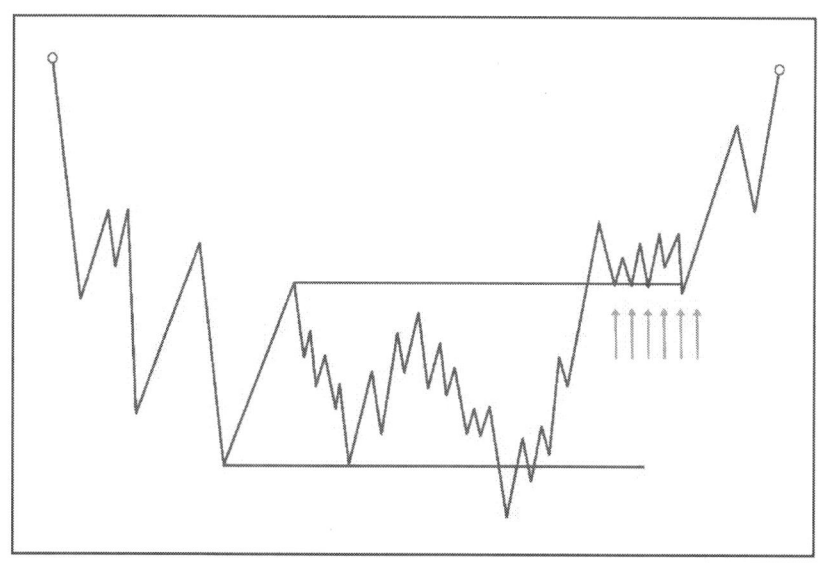

Not immediately re-entering the rank

Not immediately re-entering in the trading range

It's the most reliable sign of intentionality. We are going to look for an effective rupture that manages to stay out of range and fails in its attempts to re-enter the equilibrium zone.

In addition to observing that the movement is accompanied by an increase in price and volume ranges; and that it breaks previous control zones (previous highs and lows and minor Creek), the most powerful indication for valuing breakout as genuine is that the price manages to stay out of the range.

It denotes that there is no longer interest at lower prices and confirms that the movement is being supported by the big operators.

Representation of lack of interest

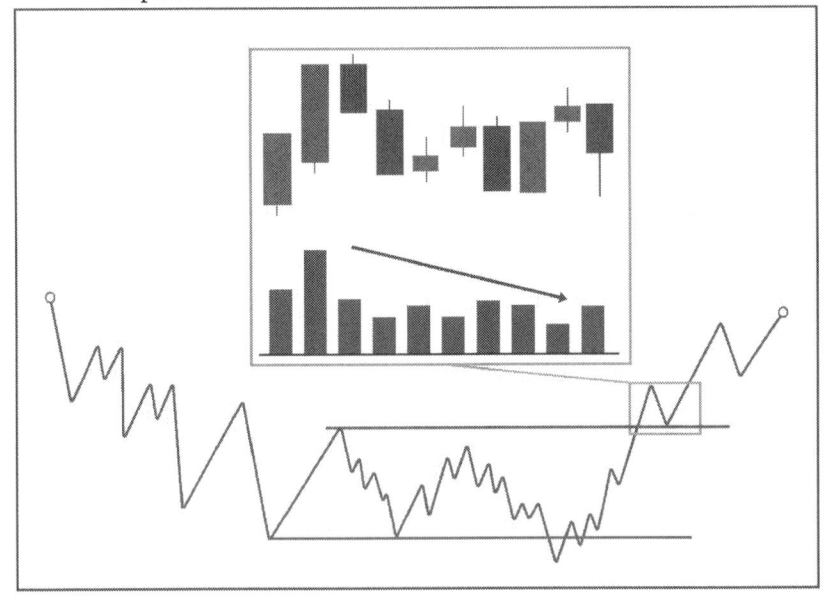

Lack of interest after bullish breakout

Another indication that would add strength to effective rupture would be to subsequently observe unintentional candles: narrow range, intertwined and with a volume smaller than that seen on the rupture movement.

Distance of the rupture

On the other hand, the distance covered by the price could be another indication to consider. Although there is no predefined distance, the distance should be obvious. In other words, the breakout that manages to move quite a few points away from the structure gives us greater confidence.

Breakout does not offer an opportunity

In operational terms, this action does not represent an operational opportunity. This is mainly because it is in a delicate area where a huge amount of cross orders will be taking place and it could change the control of the market.

What at first appears to be an effective break could turn into a Shake. And this is why it is more convenient to wait for the subsequent test with which to confirm the action definitively.

Even so, it is obviously not guaranteed that the operation will be successful. The market is an environment of constant uncertainty and is totally out of our control. As discretionary operators, all we can do is add signs that favor control on one side or the other to try to position ourselves. In the end, it is a question of probabilities.

Sign of Strength

The Sign of Strength (SOS) is an upward movement that originates in the minimum of Phase C (Spring or LPS) and ends up producing the break of the high part of the range (Creek).

All this generates the change of character prior to the start of the upward movement outside the range. It is followed by a retreat to the broken Creek to generate the BackUp to the Edge of the Creek (BUEC) action. If it fails to stay above that zone and re-enters the range, the event would be an Upthrust (UT).

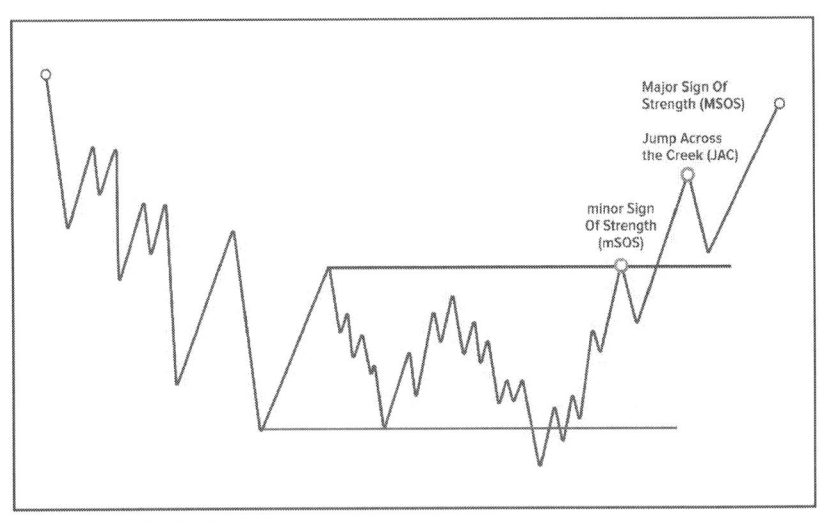

mSOS and MSOS/JAC

A great show of strength what denotes is an urgency of the institutions to enter. They are very bullish and buy aggressively.

To appreciate that we can really be before an SOS we want to see that the bullish movement has ease of movement and that it reaches the midpoint of the range. In addition, any regression now should remain above the Spring minimum to show strength.

Minor SOS

In the event that the upward movement fails to break the structure, this movement would be labeled as minor Sign of Strength (mSOS).

If during Phase B we observe a movement with SOS characteristics, we could also label this event as minor SOS.

Sign of Strength Bar

This is a bullish bar with a wide range, closing at highs and increasing volume, although it could also be a bullish gap.

It indicates the presence of strong demand for quality. It is the institutional buying point.

It could be used as an entry trigger. If in the operative area (after a shake, after a break and in trend) we observe a strength bar (SOS Bar), it is the definitive sign that the great professionals are supporting the upward movement and it provides us with a good opportunity to join in long.

Sign of Weakness

The Major Sign of Weakness (MSOW) is a strong bearish movement whose origin is in the maximum of Phase C (UTAD or LPSY) and causes the break of the lower part of the range (ICE) to start a new bearish trend.

It could be a second, third or fourth attempt to break the ICE and this is the most successful.

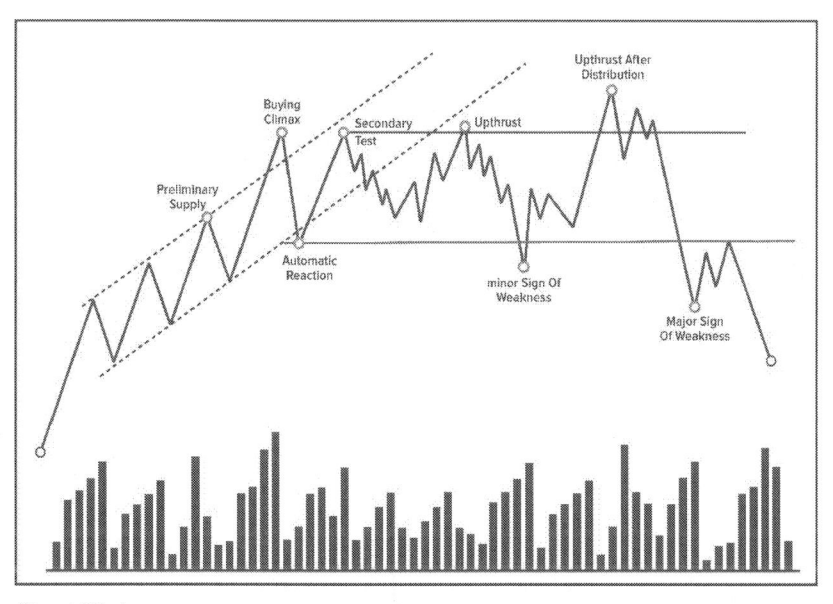

Sign of Weakness

To assess the presence of the SOW we want to see that the bearish movement moves easily, covering a relatively long distance and that at least reaches half of the structure. In addition to this, any regression should not reach the maximum set by the UTAD.

minor SOW

If after the test event in Phase C this movement of weakness is not able to break the structure, we would label it as minor Sign of Weakness (mSOW). This is a sign of minor weakness.

We could also label as such any movement that during the development of Phase B meets these characteristics in price and volume.

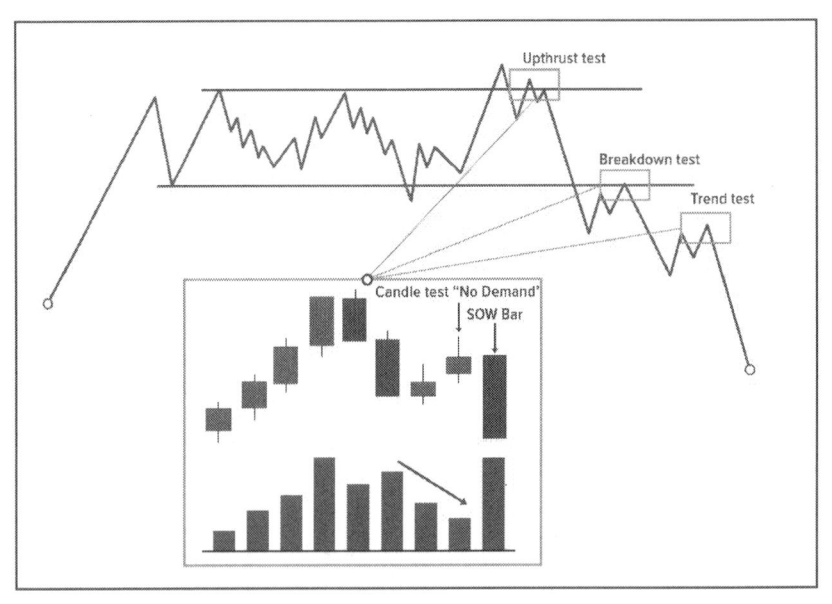

SOW Bar

Sign of Weakness Bar

Visually it is seen as a bearish bar with a relative increase in price and volume ranges and its closing at lows in the candle range, although it could also be identified by a bearish gap.

It signals the aggressiveness of the sellers and is therefore a professional point of sale.

The main use we can give it is as an entry trigger for sales operations. If in the operative zone (after a shake, after a break and in trend) we observe a bar of weakness (SOW Bar), it is the definitive signal that the great professionals are supporting the movement downwards and it provides us with a good opportunity to sell short.

Chapter 20 - Event 7: Confirmation

When the breakout event appears, it is only "potential" since the confirmation comes from your test. As with Shakes, signs of Strength or Sign of Weakness need to be tested.

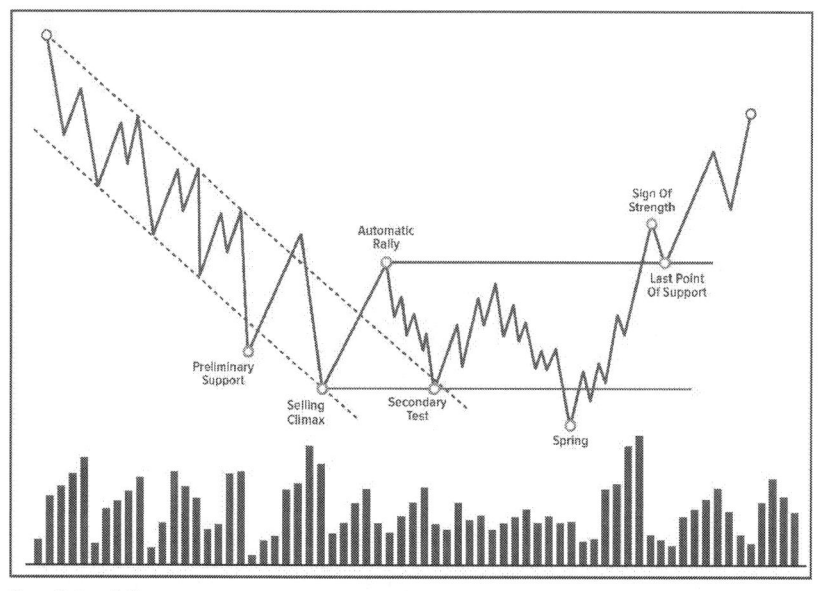

Last Point of Support

If we have a successful test, we are now in a position to label the previous move with greater confidence and the latter, your test, is the confirmation event. In other words, the test will confirm whether or not we are facing a true intentionality movement.

In terms of methodology, just as the upward rupture movement is labeled as Sign of Strength (SOS) or Jump Across the Creek (JAC), the reverse movement confirming the rupture is labeled as Last Point of Support (LPS) or Back Up to the Edge of the Creek (BUEC).

For the bearish example the break as we know it causes a sign of weakness (Sign of Weakness - SOW) and the backward movement that would confirm it is labeled as Last Point of Supply (LPSY) or Fall Through the Ice (FTI), although the latter term is less well known. We remember that the Ice is the support zone in the structures and this term comes from an analogy similar to the Creek.

But how can we know if we can wait for the confirmation event? Obviously, we can't know. It's about adding clues that make it more likely that a scenario will occur rather than the opposite one. In this case, to wait for the confirmation test we first want to see that the price makes an impulsive movement, evidenced by an expansion in the price ranges and an increase in the volume traded. At this point our main scenario should be to wait for a reversal movement to look for a trading opportunity.

How the confirmation appears on the graph

As we have already mentioned, this is the most delicate moment because it is a question of examining whether we are facing a potential event of rupture or shaking.

It is recommended to go back to the section of the previous chapter where the keys of the breakout event are commented. In this action of confirmation, we seek to make exactly what is exposed there happen:

- That the market travels a significant distance in the break-out movement.
- Let the test movement be done with narrow range, interlaced and low volume candles.

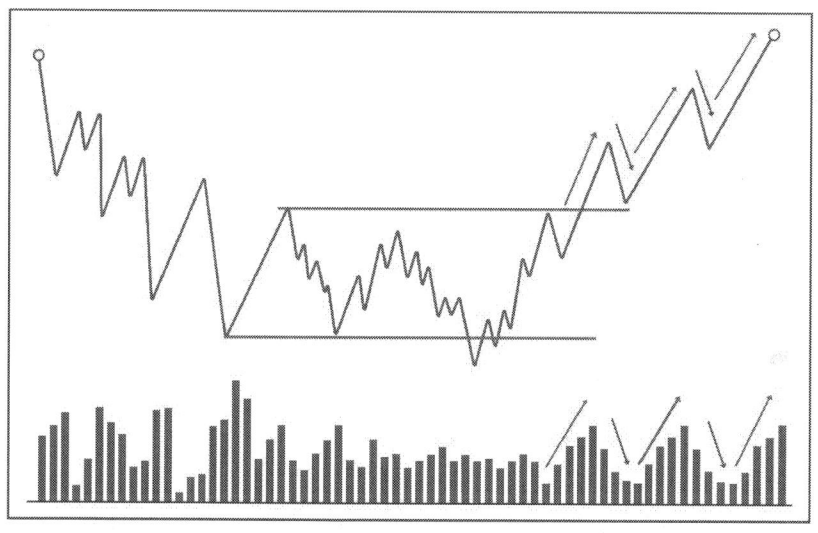

Natural action for trend movements

That the price does not re-enter the range.

As we have seen, the breakthrough movement will give us greater confidence if it is accompanied by an increase in price ranges and volume; likewise, we want to see that the reverse movement that will test the broken structure is accompanied by a decrease in price ranges and volume in comparative terms.

This is the natural action for all movements that make up a trend: impulsive movements that show intentionality and corrective movements that denote lack of interest.

Warning signal after breakout

If there is a relatively high volume on the confirmation test, it is best to proceed with caution as this volume indicates that there is latent interest in that direction.

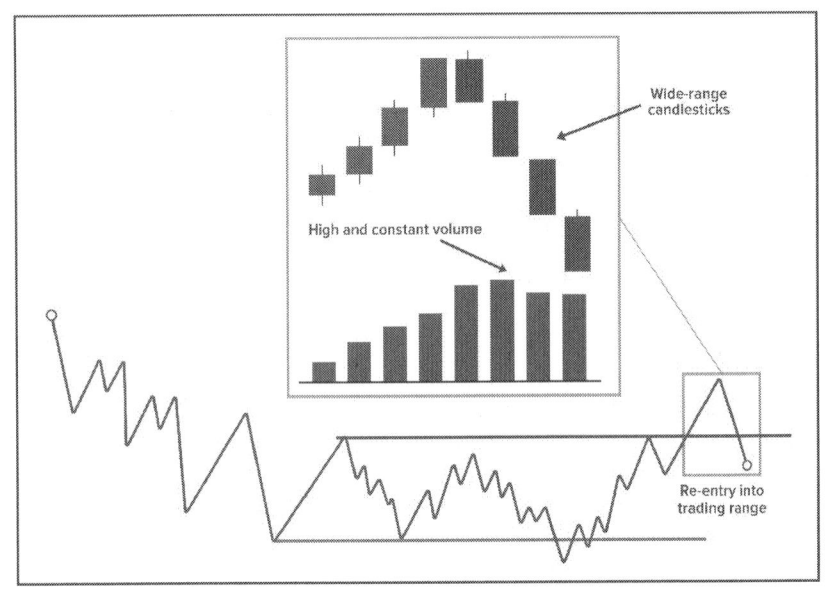

Signal alerting of possible shaking instead of breakout

And as we know, the big trader will not initiate the expected move until he has made sure that the road is free of resistance. Therefore, we should wait for successive tests to be developed over the zone.

A corrective move with wide price ranges and high volume cancels out the likelihood that the first move will be a break and most likely at this point the price will re-enter the range leaving the potential break finally as a shaking.

Operational Opportunity

This confirmation event appears in an ideal location to enter the market or to add to an open position.

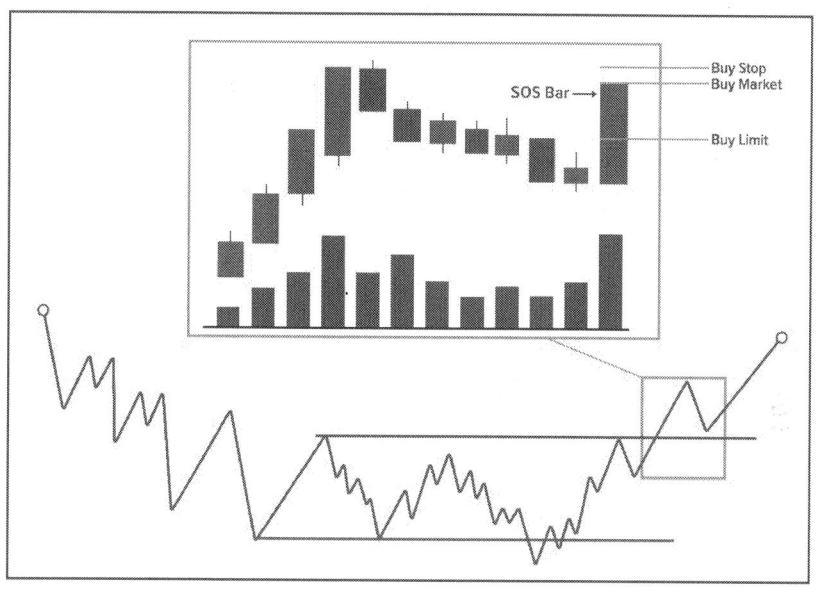

Buying Opportunity at BUEC

Originally this was the preferred position for Richard Wyckoff to enter the market because in our favor we have identified all the price action on our left where we can see the effort of professionals to carry out an accumulation or distribution campaign and therefore offers us an opportunity with a relatively lower risk.

To buy, a good option would be to wait for a fortress candle (SOSbar) to appear and place a market entry order, or a stop order at the break of the candle, or even a limited buy order at a certain level waiting for the price to fall back to it. Place or move the stop loss of the entire position under the Last Point of Support and the broken Creek.

To sell, wait for a good weakness candle (SOWbar) to appear and enter the market using the order that best suits your personality as a trader. Place or move the stop loss over the Last Point of Supply and the broken Ice line.

Quantify the entry trigger

Unfortunately, all discretionary approaches by their very nature have a great disadvantage due to the subjectivity required when carrying out analyses and presenting scenarios.

This subjectivity is the reason why methods with a real underlying logic such as the Wyckoff methodology may not be winners in the hands of all operators.

As you may have read somewhere else, human participation in a trading strategy is considered to be the weakest link, and this is obviously due to the emotional section that governs us.

To mitigate this, many recommend trying to objectify our trading strategy as much as possible. But this is not a simple task, much less for Wyckoff traders. There are so many elements to bear in mind when considering scenarios that it would seem impossible to create a strategy with 100% objective rules that always operates in the same way.

One solution that is in our hands is to try to quantify the trigger that we will use to enter the market. It is undoubtedly a simple measure that can help us to incorporate some objectivity into our strategy.

If you are only trading using bars or candles, you may want to quantify what happens when a certain price pattern appears. For example, to buy, we could quantify a simple price turn composed of a bearish candlestick followed by a bullish candlestick. And from there we can complicate it as much as we want. We can add other variables such as that some moving average is below, that the second bullish candle is higher than a number of pips, that a stop purchase order is used at the break of the candle and so on.

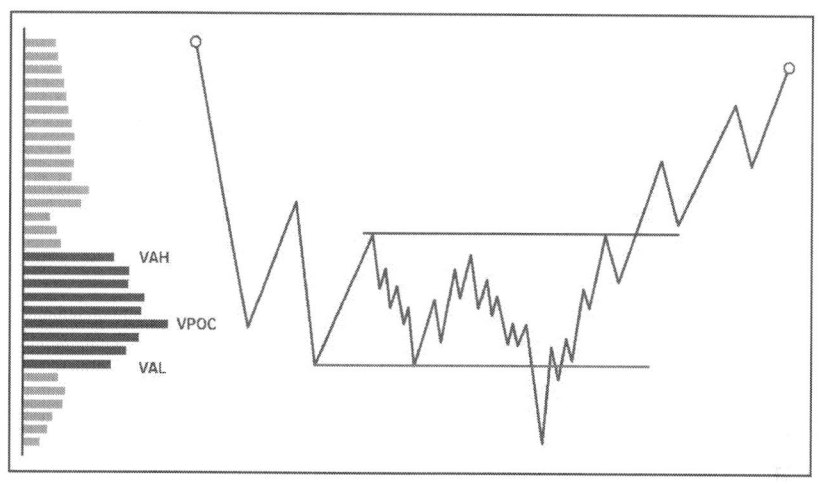

Example of Volume Profile

If you are also trading using volume based tools, you may want to add other variables such as the price being above the POC (Point of Control), VAH (Value Area High), VAL (Value Area Low) or VWAP (Volume Weighted Average Price); or that the bull candle is also accompanied by a significant increase in the Delta (Difference between Bid and Ask).

The options are endless, from the simplest to the most complex; the only limit is our creativity. But this is hard work because if you don't know how to do it through code (programming a robot), you will have to do it by hand and this will require a lot of time. In addition, when doing a Backtest you have to take into account other aspects such as data quality, expenses in commissions (spreads, commission, swap), latency problems (slippage), as well as other points concerning the optimization of strategies.

Last Point of Support

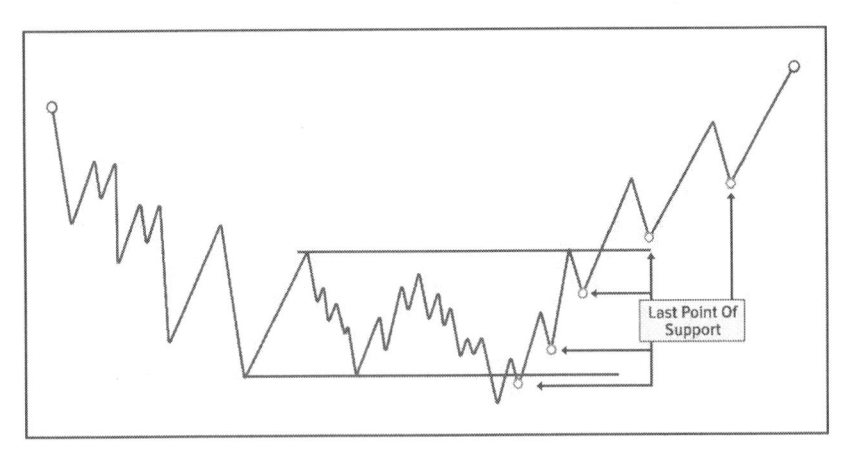

Last Point of Support Types

The Last Point of Support (LPS) is the immediate action that precedes a Sign of Strength (SOS). It is an attempt by sellers to push the price lower but fails when buyers aggressively appear, giving rise to a new bullish momentum.

Based on the movement that precedes the Last Point of Support, we can find different types:

- Last Point of Support after shaking. In case the price comes from developing a Spring/Shakeout, the Last Point of Support would be the test of those two events.
- Last Point of Support within the range. If the price comes from developing a Sign of Strength, the Last Point of Support will appear in the bearish reversal.
- Last Point of Support out of range. Here we have on the one hand the test movement after the break (the confirmation event, the Back Up to the Edge of the Creek); and on the other hand, all the setbacks we found during the uptrend Phase out of range.

As we know that the market moves by waves; after the bullish impulse (Sign of Strength) we expect a bearish retrocession (Last Point of Support). This retracement is the last point of support for demand. It is a price point where buyers appear to stop the fall, generating a higher minimum. This higher minimum is a previous stop before starting with a new upward impulsive movement.

Many traders guided by their lack of understanding will be buying during the development of the strength signal (SOS). But this action is not correct, it is best to wait for the next reaction (LPS) at that point to start looking for a trigger to enter the market.

Sometimes the Last Point of Support will occur at the same price level on which the Preliminary Support appeared because that's where the big operators started buying the asset.

Last Point of Supply

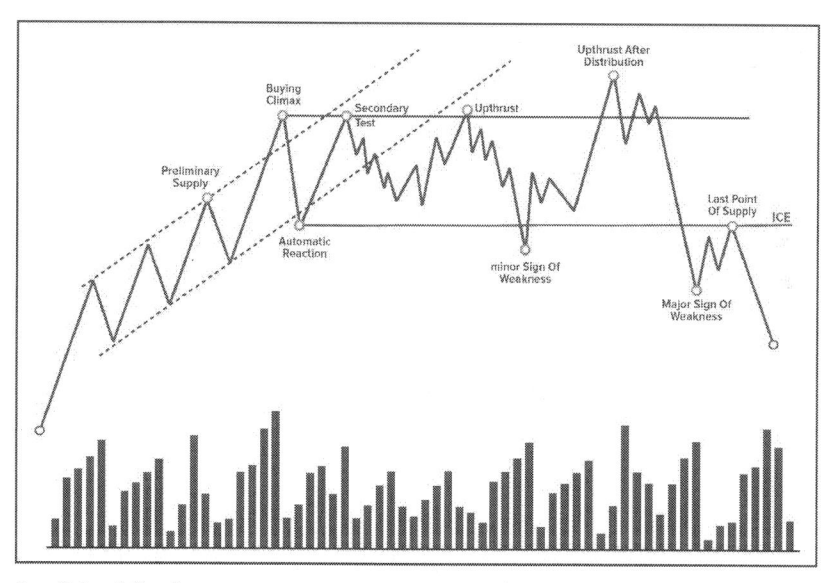

Last Point of Supply

The Last Point of Supply (LPSY) is the immediate action that precedes a Sign of Weakness (SOW). This is an attempt to raise the price but is blocked by the big sellers, who are already positioned short and appear again to protect their positions.

Based on the movement that precedes the Last Point of Supply, we can find different types:
- Last Point of Supply after shock. In case the price comes from developing an Uptrust After Distribution, the Last Point of Supply would be its test.
- Last Point of Supply within the range. If the price comes from developing a Sign of Weakness, the Last Point of Supply will appear in the bullish retreat.
- Last Point of Supply out of range. Here we have on the one hand the test movement after the break (the confirmation event, the Fall Through the Ice); and on the other hand, all the setbacks we found during the downtrend Phase out of range.

After breakout the Ice (support) with a sign of weakness (Sign of Weakness), we want to see an upward movement with narrow price ranges, which would denote the difficulty of the market to keep rising. Preferably we will expect the volume to be low, indicating a lack of interest from buyers; but we have to be careful because a high volume could signal an increase in selling interest by shorting the zone.

Last Point of Supply are good places to start or add short positions as they are the last distribution waves before a new bearish momentum begins.

The price reached in the Last Point of Supply will sometimes coincide with the level above which the Preliminary Supply appeared. This is so because if the structure is distributive, it is on the Preliminary Supply where the distribution initially began.

Part 6 - Phases

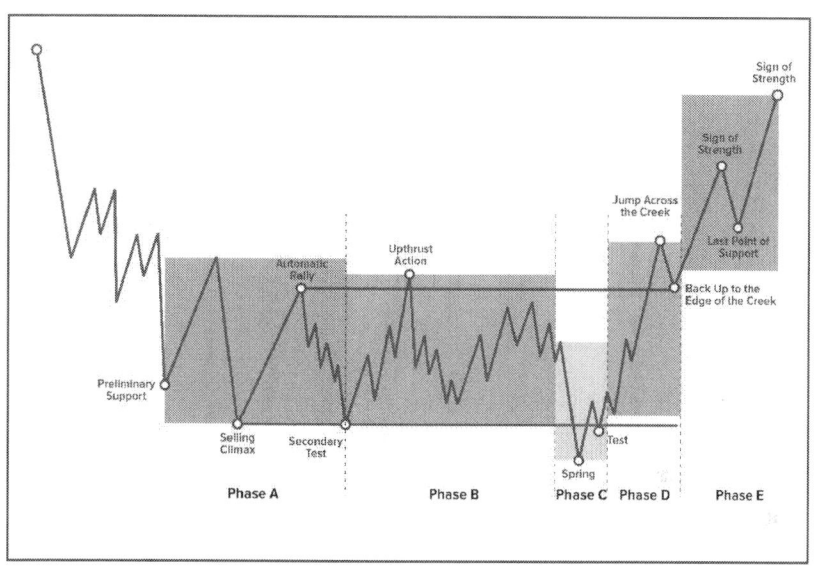

Phases

Phase analysis helps us to structure the processes of accumulation and distribution, providing us with the general context of the market. Once the general context is identified, we will be predisposed to wait for one thing to happen rather than another.

Context is a very important feature of the Wyckoff methodology, and gives it an important advantage over other technical analysis approaches. For example, a trader based on traditional technical analysis may see a resistance and seek to enter short over that area expecting a market turn; and on the other hand, a Wyckoff trader who has correctly identified the Phases may have established a greater probability that the price will effectively break that resistance and may even consider buying while waiting for the start of the uptrend outside the range.

Within the Wyckoff methodology we have five Phases: from A to E; and each of them has a unique function:

- Phase A. Stopping the previous trend.
- Phase B. Building the cause.
- Phase C. Test.
- Phase D. Trend within range.
- Phase E. Trend out of range.

By analyzing price and volume we will be able to correctly identify when they start and end. It is very important that the analysis so far is correct because it will be the only way to take advantage of the message that underlies its development.

The Phases are based on the fact that all campaigns (accumulations and distributions) require a certain amount of time until they are completed. During this time, the price develops the structures we already know. The power of Phase analysis lies in the fact that these structures generally follow repetitive patterns in their development. This means that, if we are able to correctly identify what is happening (accumulating or distributing), we will be closer to presenting scenarios with a greater probability of success.

Chapter 21 - Phase A:
Stopping the previous trend

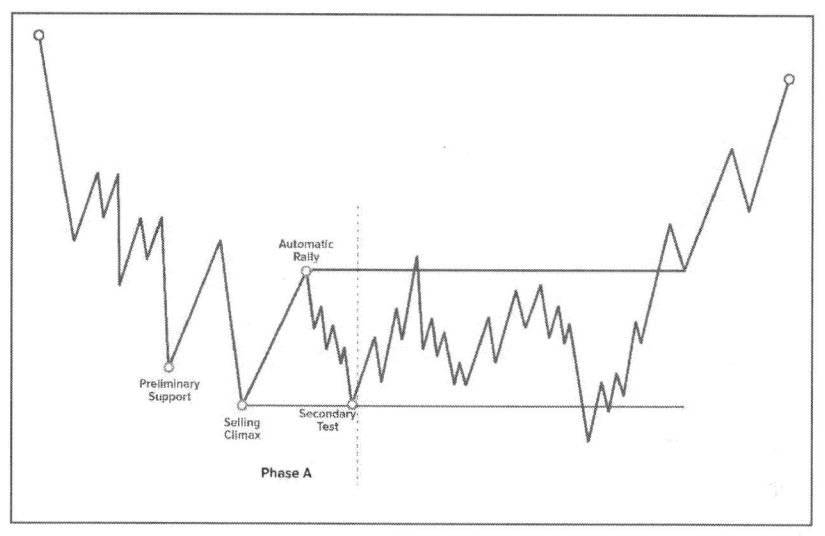

Phase A: Stopping the previous trend

The main function of this Phase is to stop the previous trend movement and return the market to a state of equilibrium between the forces of supply and demand, or between buyers and sellers. We move from a trend context to a range context.

Phase A consists of the first four events:

- Preliminary Support and Preliminary Supply
- Selling Climax and Buying Climax
- Automatic Rally and Automatic Reaction
- Secondary Test

Prior to the start of this first Phase, the market is controlled on either side. As we know, a control of the sellers will be represented as a downtrend; and a control of the buyers as an uptrend.

The price may be reaching interesting levels where the big trader begins to see value. In other words, they see a potential profit with the difference they have found between the value they give and the current price. It is time to start developing the stock absorption campaign.

But we will not be able to identify this signal of true interest until the first events of the methodology appear. The **Preliminary Stop** with its peak volume already alerts us to an increase in participation and a possible massive closure of positions. The most likely thing is that the big traders have begun to glimpse an overextended condition in the price and begin to take profits.

The **Climax**, which as we know can also appear without climatic volume (Selling Exhaustion and Buying Exhaustion), identifies us one of the extremes of the structure and its action is very relevant to finish exhausting those who until then maintained control of the market.

The appearance of the **Reaction** is one of the most informative events because it confirms that something is happening. The price came previously in a prolonged trend and this reaction is the first time that it lets see with relative significance that there begins to be an interest in the other side.

The **Test** puts an end to this first Phase by starting the development of Phase B from there.

Chapter 22 - Phase B: Building the Cause

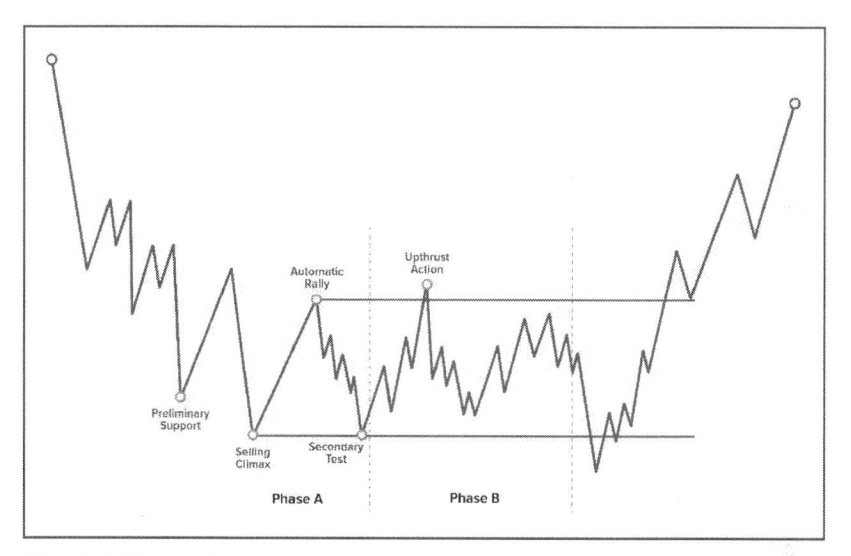

Phase B: Building the Cause

After the Secondary Test the Phase B begins, whose intention is the construction of the cause with the objective of preparing the subsequent effect.

Phase B consists of successive tests (Secondary Test in B) that can be performed at both the upper and lower ends of the structure:

- Upthrust Action and Upthrust
- Secondary Test as Sign of Weakness and minor Sign of Weakness

During this phase, the market is in equilibrium and this is where the great professionals take advantage to absorb most of the stock they need before the end of the season.

In proportional terms, we want this Phase to be greater than Phases A and C. This is a general guideline because, although there will be occasions when the Phases will be of equal or even shorter duration (such as in a hypodermic action or V turn), it is most likely that we will find that this type of temporal proportionality is met.

If this proportionality is not met, i.e. Phase B has a shorter duration than Phase A or C, this will denote an urgency on the part of the operators who are absorbing the stock and adds greater strength to the trend movement that follows.

Chapter 23 - Phase C: Test

Phase C begins with the start of the jerk movement and ends after the jerk test.

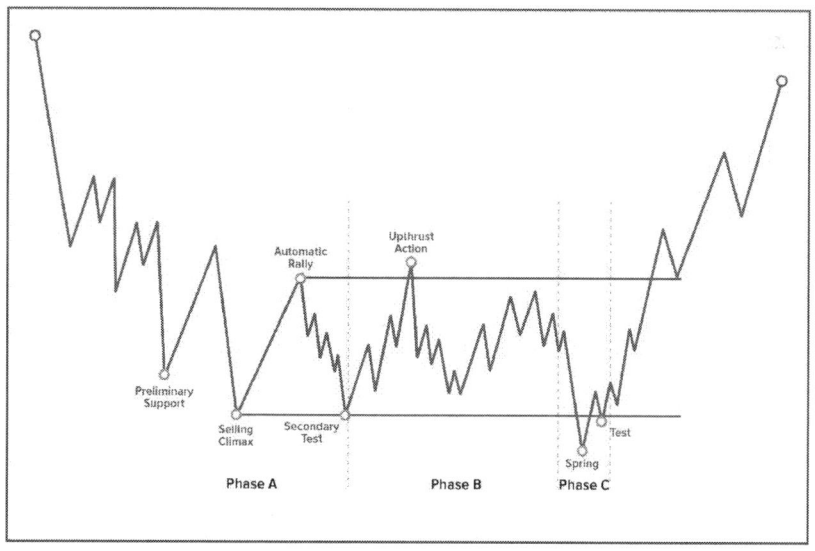

Phase C: Test

In this phase, the great professional checks the level of interest that the rest of the market participants have on certain price levels.

It is made up of the Shaking event:

- Spring/Shakeout
- UpThrust After Distribution (UTAD)

Before starting the trend movement, it is most likely that they will develop this Shake action in order to verify that there are virtually no traders willing to enter the opposite direction and that therefore the path of least resistance is in their favor.

If they observe a high participation in that zone, this means that they have not yet absorbed all the available stock and that therefore the control of the market is not yet unbalanced towards one of the sides (buyers or sellers).

Under this circumstance, it is most likely that either the large operators will give up the campaign, continuing the price in this case in the same direction as the prevailing trend; or Phase B will continue to be extended until there is complete absorption of all this available stock, producing an imbalance in favour of professionals. In this case, the price will need to carry out successive tests in this area until the lack of interest is verified.

A very important aspect to bear in mind that can happen at this stage is that the shaking event will not necessarily sweep the ends of the structure. Doing so is ideal because the greater this movement, the more liquidity you will have been able to capture and therefore the more "gasoline" the subsequent movement will have.

But it can also be the case that a Shake takes place without reaching the extremes. We would still be before the Test event in Phase C and we could label this action as Spring/Upthrust minor, or Spring/Upthrust in function of Last Point of Support/Supply.

In any case and as I usually repeat, the labels "is the least". We have to think in functional terms and what really interests us is to know what is happening. It is of little use to us to know how the methodology labels market actions if we do not know in depth what lies behind them.

Chapter 24 - Phase D: Trend within range

The beginning of this Phase is after the end of the shock test and until the confirmation event is fully developed.

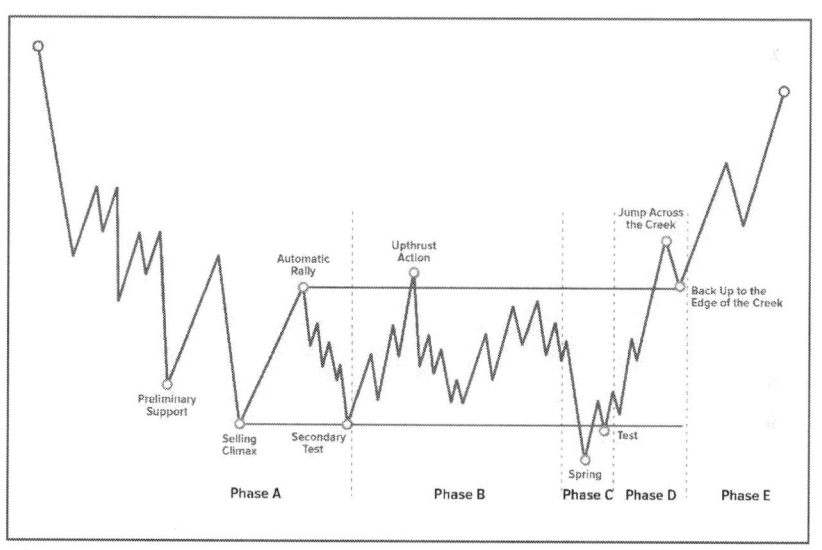

Phase D. Trend within range

    Without opposition to sight, the path of least resistance is clear. The market is in imbalance and this is observed in the graph through the development of the Break event.

Phase D consists of the **Breakout** and **Confirmation** events:
- Sign of Strength/Jump Across the Creek and Sign of Weakness
- Last Point of Support/Back Up to the Edge of the Creek and Last Point of Supply

If we are correct in the analysis, after the key Shake event, the price should now develop a clear trend movement within the range with wide candles and increased volume to cause the effective breakdown of the structure.

That zone that establishes the Reaction event (Creek or Ice) is the last barrier that must be overcome to conclude that one side has final control. If the price reaches that area and there is too much opposition (there are still many traders willing to trade against this movement), we are left with two possible scenarios.

On the one hand, the price may fall back again by developing a Last Point of Support/Supply within the range before attacking that area again (it would be something like taking a run to jump the river); or on the other hand, those large traders who have previously built the campaign may decide to pay the price it will cost them to cross that area and start from there the breakout movement, absorbing all those orders at a worse price.

We would still have to be alert to a third possible scenario, which would be that this attempt at rupture fails and develops in it a new shock, a new Test in Phase C that would cause the effective rupture towards the opposite side.

If the price has developed structurally as planned, this last possibility should be the least likely to happen, but we must be aware of it and keep it in mind. What happens in this case is simply that higher forces have been absorbing in the opposite direction; developing a much more discreet absorption campaign.

We must bear in mind that the market is a struggle between great professionals, between funds and institutions with all kinds of interests. An important point to make is that not all institutions operating in the financial markets make money. The truth is that a large number of them are just as much losers as the vast majority of retail operators. These losing institutions are the favorite victims of the big operators as they handle significant amounts of capital.

If the breakout develops relatively easily, and the signals leaving the price and volume so indicate, then we will look for the confirmation event to unfold.

For this one, as we have already commented, it is essential that the price endures on the other side of the structure and does not generate an immediate re-entry. Besides this, we will look for that test movement to be generated with little interest.

Chapter 25 - Phase E: Trend out of range

This Phase starts after the confirmation event.

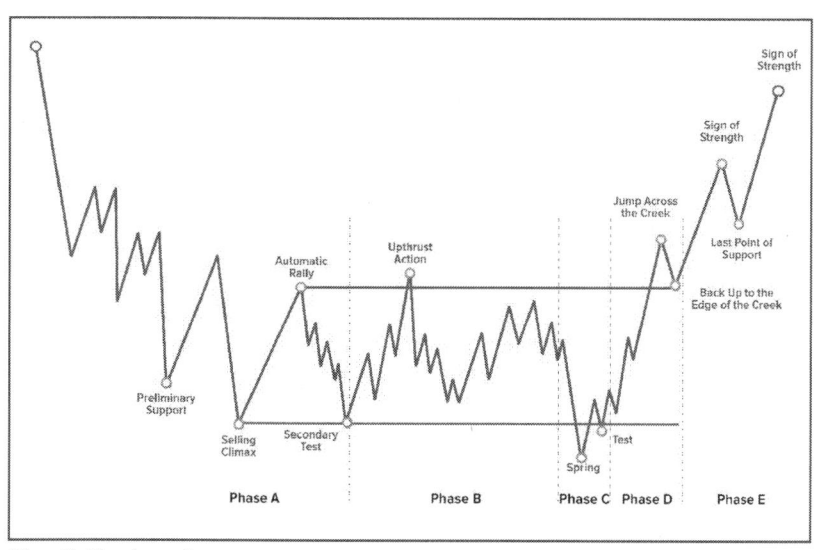

Phase E. Trend out of range

If the test after the break was successful and no traders appeared in the opposite direction, it can definitely be confirmed that one side has absolute control of the market and therefore we should only seek to trade in that direction.

This Phase consists of a succession of impulsive and reactive movements:
- Sign of Strength and Sign of Weakness
- Last Point of Support and Last Point of Supply

The price abandons the structure upon which the cause has been built previously and begins a trend as an effect of the same. This fact of successful break + confirmation is the great warning that great professionals are positioned in that direction.

It is from this point on that we must implement all the tools for evaluating trends.

Part 7 - Trading

Our trading and investment decisions will be based on the three elements that I believe are most important to consider in the discretionary reading of charts, in order: the context, the structures and the operating areas.

1. The context

It has to do mainly with what is on the left of the chart, both in the time frame you decide to trade and in some higher time frame.

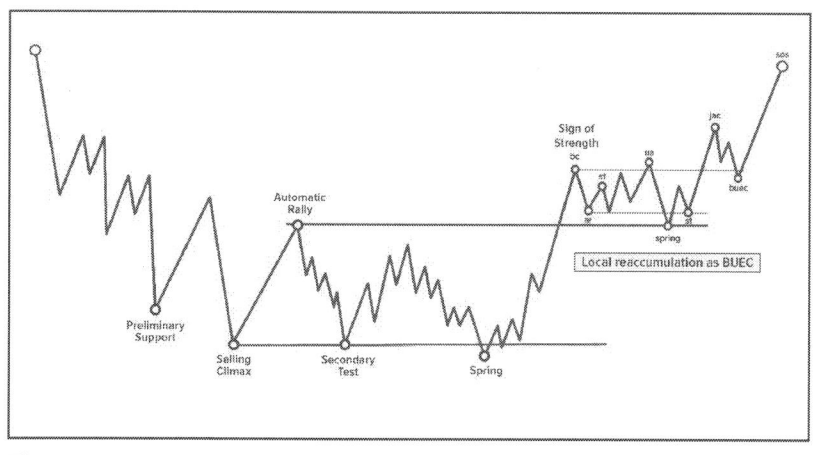

The importance of context

The vital rule regarding context is clear: operate in favor of the larger structure. This means that, as markets develop multiple structures at the same time but in different temporalities, we must always prioritize the development of the longer-term structure. This is the most logical way for us to bias the direction of the market.

For example, if we find ourselves after the upward break in a potential accumulation structure of a higher time frame, over that area we will favor the development of a smaller reaccumulation structure that will act according to BUEC of the larger structure.

In this example, we see how our analysis has been biased (favouring the development of a reaccumulation) based on what the price was doing until it reached that point (the potential main accumulation structure). This is the importance of context.

In addition to providing us with more secure trading opportunities, identifying the context also helps us not to look for trades on the wrong side of the market.

In other words, if our structural analysis tells us that the market could be accumulating, from that moment on we will only try to look for buy trades; discarding outright the sell trades.

This is very important as eventually we may not be able to find our way into the current upward movement, but at least we will avoid being positioned on the wrong side of the market, which in this example would be the short side. We will not be able to win, but at least we will not lose.

2. The structures

It is the cornerstone of the Wyckoff methodology. Our task is to try to understand what is happening within the structures, who is gaining control between buyers and sellers.

The only objective of internalizing all the theory seen so far is to arrive at this point in the operation to pose scenarios as robust as possible.

Many are the operators who underestimate the Wyckoff methodology's approach, alluding to the fact that it was developed under very different market conditions than the current ones. This is absolutely true since the technologies available at the end of the

20th century, as well as the structure of the market itself, have changed considerably with respect to more modern times.

What has not changed is that in the end it is about the interaction between supply and demand. Regardless of the source that executes the orders of the participants, this interaction leaves its mark on the price in the form of structures that repeat themselves continuously.

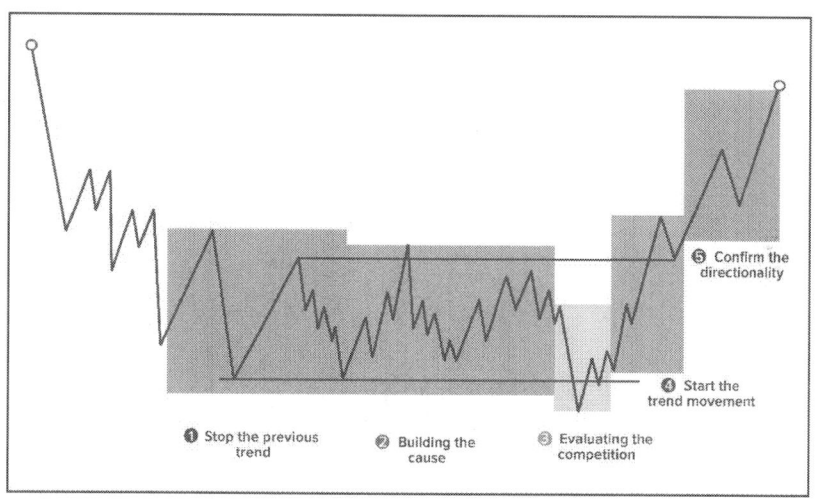

The importance of structures

The logic of the structures is based on the fact that, in order for the price to be rotated, it needs to be accumulated or distributed in a protocol that requires time and is developed systematically. Although markets sometimes cause aggressive V-turns, this is not the norm and we should therefore focus on the complete development of the structures.

This protocol roughly follows a series of steps (phases and events of the methodology) that allow us to know when the price is likely to be turned. In summary, these steps are:

1. Stop the previous trend
2. Building the cause
3. Evaluating the competition
4. Start the trend movement
5. Confirm the directionality

What the Wyckoff methodology has done is put a magnifying glass on each of these steps and create a discipline whose objective is to evaluate the footprints left by the interaction of supply and demand on price and volume to discern where market control is most likely to be imbalanced. This is the task of the Wyckoff trader.

But back to the beginning, the objective is to pose solid scenarios; and this will be impossible if we do not know all the elements that make up the methodology.

3. Operational areas

The underlying principle is auction theory and the market's need to facilitate trading. We have discussed this previously. Large traders need to find other traders with whom they can place orders when opening and closing trades (counterparty). That is why they take advantage of the Shake movements to open positions, and keep them until they reach certain levels where they will again find enough liquidity to close those positions.

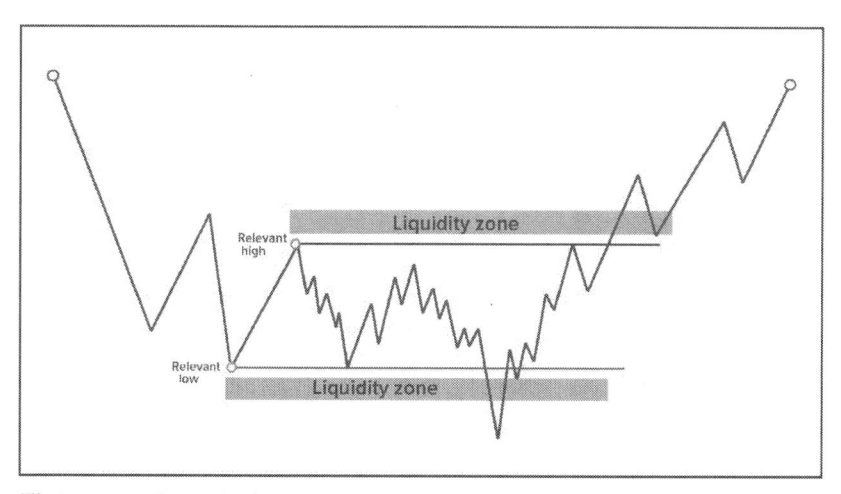

The importance of operational zones

The key is that these operating zones act as price magnets because they generate enough interest to make different traders want to place their pending orders on them (attracting liquidity). And this liquidity is what makes the price tend to come to them.

For example, large traders who have bought heavily on a bearish move (Spring), will need to keep the position open at least until they find another major liquidity zone that allows them to close those purchases. Since they now want to take profit (close buy positions = sell), they need volume buyers; traders willing to buy their sell orders.

That is why they almost obligatorily need to visit these zones/levels in which there are a large amount of pending orders to be executed (liquidity); allowing us to indirectly take advantage of this information. Later on, we will go deeper into some of these levels in particular.

Chapter 26 - Primary positions

Within the methodology, the only areas on which a possible operation will be assessed are very well defined: In Phase C, in the zone of potential shock; in Phase D, during the development of the tendential movement within the range and in the test after the break; and in Phase E looking for tests in tendency or minor structures in favor of the major structure (context).

We are going to detail the different zones on which we will look to operate, as well as the different events that can occur within them.

When comparing the advantages and disadvantages between the different operating positions, the key is that the greater the development of the structure, the greater the confidence we will have in the operations, but the lower the potential benefit due to this. It would be the same thing to say that, the sooner we get the signals, the greater the potential travel and the lower the reliability.

In Phase C

This is the position that offers us the best Risk:Reward ratio since we are at one end of the structure and the potential movement is relatively large.

The negative part of entering this location is that they are less precise entries since until that moment the development of the range has had a shorter duration in comparison with the other two operative positions.

Entry into the shake

Only recommended if the shaking is done with a relatively low volume. As we know, high volumes tend to be tested to verify the commitment of those operators, so it is more sensible to wait for a new visit to that area.

With this in mind it would not make much sense to go directly into a shake that has developed with a lot of volume when they are most likely to develop such a test. And normally this test will be able to give us an even better Risk:Reward ratio.

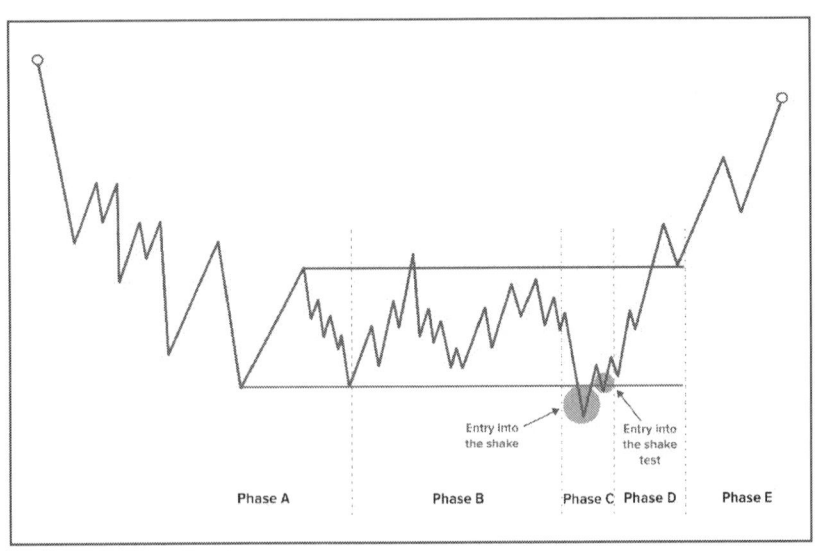

Accumulation Phase C entries

Shakes are easily identifiable as they occur at the ends of the structure. It would not be necessary to monitor the development of the range minute by minute, it would be enough to place some alerts when the price crosses these extremes and we will be in predisposition to operate them.

Entry into the shake test

It's one of every Wyckoff operator's favorite tickets. After the shock, expect a new visit over the area with narrowing ranges and decreasing volume (see Event #4: Test).

One of the important points of this test is that it should be kept and not make a new extreme. In other words, for the example of the Spring test, it should remain above the minimum established by the Spring. For the example of the Upthrust test, it should stay below the maximum set by the Upthrust.

Entry into the Last Point of Support

This type of entry is much more difficult to see since we only know that it is the last point of support after the actual breakage of the structure (Basic accumulation scheme #2)

Phase C can be generated either with a Shake or with this last foothold event (LPS/LPSY). Thanks to the action of the Shake itself (sweeping of a previous liquidity zone at the end of the structure) we know when the structure is developing. This is very different with the last support point, since we cannot know at any time when this event may be developing, being in many cases inoperable.

In Phase D

If the Shake + test are successful, we should now see a sign of intent that will lead to the price in the opposite direction. This is the context we will work with.

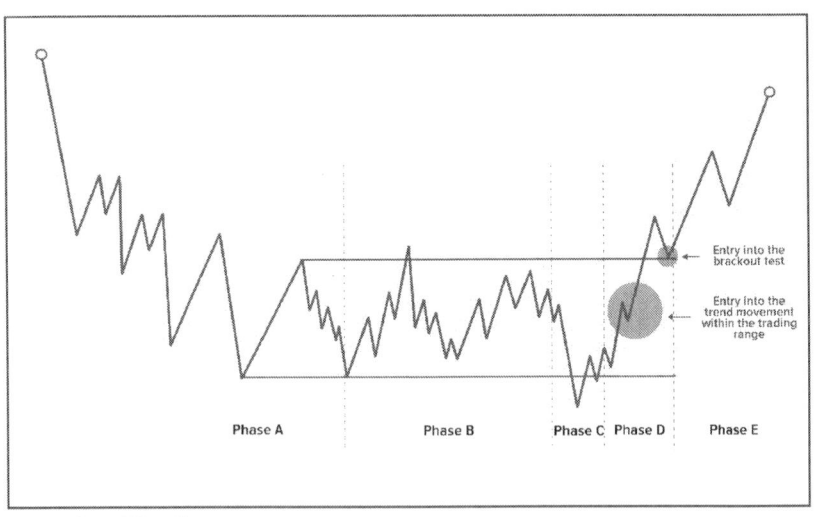

Accumulation Phase D entries

In order to benefit from this approach, we have different ways to enter the market.

Entry into the trend movement within the range
During the trip of the price from one end to the other can offer us different possibilities of entry.

<u>With a significant bar</u>

One of them would be to wait for the appearance of new intentional sails (SOS/SOW bar). This is the definitive sign of professional interest. If during the development of that trend movement within the range we observe good trend candles, they are still very interesting opportunities to enter the market.

<u>With minor structure</u>

Another way to incorporate would be to look for some minor structure in favor of the directionality of the shock. For example, if we have just identified a Spring + test, we may be able to go down in the middle of the structure to look for a minor structure of reaccumulation that would give us the trigger to buy. In the bearish example, if we identify an Upthrust + test, we could go down in temporality from there and look for minor redistribution structures to go up in the bearish trend movement.

With a minor Shake

Finally, in this area of the structure we could also look for minor shaking. They are called minor because they do not occur over the entire ends of the structure. This is another very good way to enter in case you do not want to go down in time and look for a minor structure. Actually, the pattern of the minor shock and the minor structure is the same, although the minor structure would offer a better Risk:Reward ratio.

Both minor structures and minor shocks should be labeled as the last support point (LPS/LPSY) since they are turns in favor of the tendential movement that occurs within the structure.

Entry into the break test (Confirmation Event No. 7)

As we discussed in the chapter dealing with this event, it was Richard Wyckoff's favorite operating position because of everything the chart could tell him up to that point.

The potential for establishing profit taking is less, but instead we have on the left all the development of the structure, which gives us a greater probability that we will position ourselves along with the great professionals and in favor of the least resistance.

In Phase E

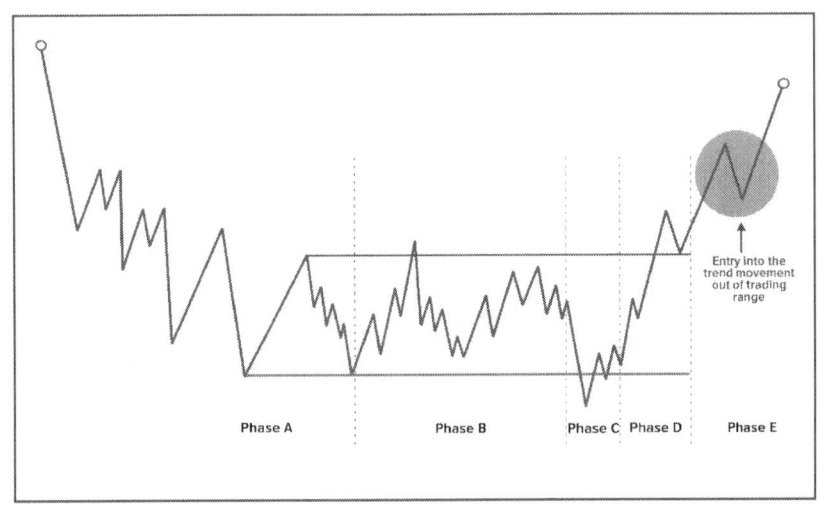

Accumulation Phase E entries

After the confirmation that we are facing an effective break and imminent start of the out-of-range trend movement, we must now focus on looking for operational opportunities in favour of the preceding accumulation/distribution.

This type of operations is the most "secure" since we are positioned in favor of the last accumulation or distribution. However, the disadvantage is that the potential path is smaller, although it will depend on the amount of cause that has been built up during the structure.

Entry into the out-of-range trend movement

As with the operations in the Phase D trend environment, we can assess different possibilities for entering the market:

<u>With a significant bar</u>

Sometimes the market will move in a very volatile environment and this speed is likely to leave us with no possibility of entering the market if we are waiting for the perfect entry.

To try to mitigate this, we could enter in favour of movement simply after the appearance of new intentionality candles (SOS/SOW bar).

There are quite a few signals in favour of such a move, so a new appearance of this type of candle that indicates professional intervention may be the perfect excuse to place our orders in the market.

<u>Entry with minor structures</u>

If the main structure that we have previously identified is in a time frame of 4 hours or 1 day, it could be interesting to go down to a time frame of 1 hour or less to look there for the development of a smaller structure that would allow us to incorporate in favour of the trend movement.

This means that if we have a macro structure of accumulation underneath, the most interesting thing to do in order to go up to the upward movement would be to go down in temporality and look for a minor structure of reaccumulation.

Similarly, if what the market shows is a main distribution structure above the current price, the most advisable thing to do would be to go down in time and look for a minor redistribution structure.

Entry with a shake

It should be treated exactly the same as the Shake entry in Phase C. It is the same event with the only difference being the location where it takes place.

The methodology distinguishes these Shake events depending on the location. When they occur in the middle of the favorable trend movement it is called Ordinary Shakeout and Ordinary Upthrust.

In addition to the difference in location, these types of shocks may appear with less preparation of the continuation structure (reaccumulation or redistribution) because the market is already in motion.

As we have mentioned, the operation in Phase E would be the safest between quotes because we are positioning ourselves in favour of the last accumulation or distribution already confirmed. And we know that until at least the first events of a Phase A stop of the previous trend are developed, the most logical thing is to think about a continuity of the current movement.

Summary table of trading opportunities

Direction	Phase C			Phase D		Phase E
	At the shake	At the shake test	At the last support point	At the trend movement within the trading range	At the break test	At the trend movement out of trading range
Buy	Spring #3	Spring test #1 & #2	Last Point of Support	• Sign Of Strength bar • minor structure of reaccumulation • minor Spring	Last Point of Support Candlestick test "No Supply"	• Sign Of Strength bar • minor structure of reaccumulation • Ordinary Shakeout
Sell	Uptrust without volume	Upthrust test	Last Point of Supply	• Sign Of Weakness bar • minor structure of redistribution • minor Upthrust	Last Point of Supply Candlestick test "No Demand"	• Sign Of Weakness bar • minor structure of redistribution • Ordinary Upthrust

Summary table of trading opportunities

Chapter 27 - Decision-making

Everything studied so far has had the sole objective of preparing us to arrive in the best conditions at the critical moment of every trader: the final decision making.

Once we have identified the areas we are going to wait for the price and the possible scenarios we want to see before acting, we are going to detail in depth some concepts more typical of the operation.

The main objective of internalizing this type of concept is to incorporate a certain objectivity in the reading of the graphs and, more importantly, in our operations.

The concept of the significant bar

It is difficult to determine when the price will make a market turn in the short term. The easiest way to determine it is through confirmation: confirmation that a trade has been completed.

It is a matter of identifying the presence of the institutions in the short term that enter to force that turn in the price. An example of this type of bar is those previously presented as SOSbar (Sign of Strength Bar) and SOWbar (Sign of Weakness Bar)

The characteristic of a significant bar is:
- Relatively wider range than the range of previous sails.

- A volume operated according to that total range, i.e. higher.
- Close in the middle of the total range of the bar in the direction of the current movement.
    - For a significant bullish bar close in the upper half of its range.
    - For a significant bearish bar close in the lower half of its range.
- Commitment in the direction of the current movement.
    - For a significant bullish bar the bar's close must be above some previous resistance level.

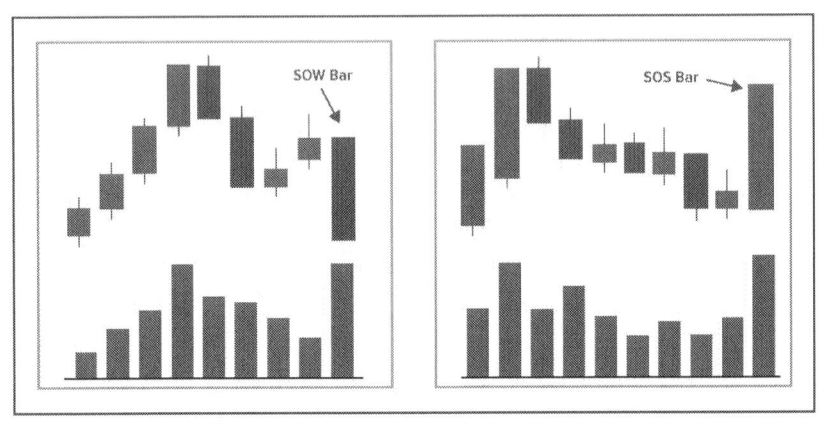

SOW bar and SOS bar

For a significant bearish bar the bar's close should be below a previous support level.

A bar with these characteristics denotes intent and will generally be associated with institutional presence. Since we assume institutional presence, we expect the price to continue to move in that direction.

If the price does not clearly develop a significant bar, we can mark two normal bars and build with them a significant bar using the same characteristics.

It is highly recommended to use this concept of significant bar to try to identify the turns of the market.

The concept of reversal of movement

Determining the end of a longer movement is not easy. The goal is to identify as early as possible the point at which the beginning of a movement in the opposite direction is likely to occur.

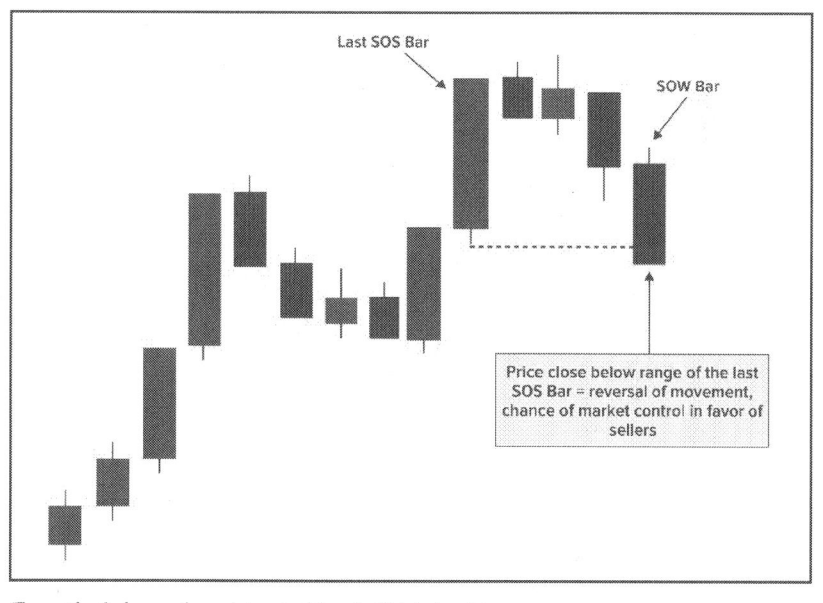

Example of change of market control from bullish to bearish

The first thing to do is to identify the last significant bar of the movement in which the price currently stands. And let's assume that this marks the current market control since the probability is that the price will continue in that direction (in the direction of whoever has control of the market).

That is, if the price is in the middle of a rising movement and above a significant rising bar, we will assume that the buyers have control of the market; and conversely, if the price is in the middle of a falling movement and below a significant falling bar, we will say that the sellers have control of the market.

With the appearance of new significant bars in favor of the movement, the control of the market will continue to shift, anchoring itself to those new significant bars.

The key is that we will determine that the control of the market has been turned around when the price breaks the last significant bar that marks the control of the market with another significant bar of inverse intentionality to the current movement.

To do this, we mark the ends of the total range of that last significant bar and a close in the opposite direction would alert us to a possible reversal of the movement:

- To determine the end of a rising movement and possible beginning of another falling one we need to see that a falling reversal bar closes below the minimum of the rising significant bar that until then marked the buyers' control.
- To determine the end of a downward movement and possible beginning of a upward one we need to see that a bullish reversal bar closes above the maximum of the significant downward bar that until then marked the control of the sellers.

This concept of movement reversals is very important because when we observe a change in character, we will probably see those reversal bars.

After the Selling Climax, we will probably see that upward reversal bar. And once the upward movement has started, we will probably see that downward reversal bar that will alert us to the end of the Automatic Rally. And so on with all the events in the range.

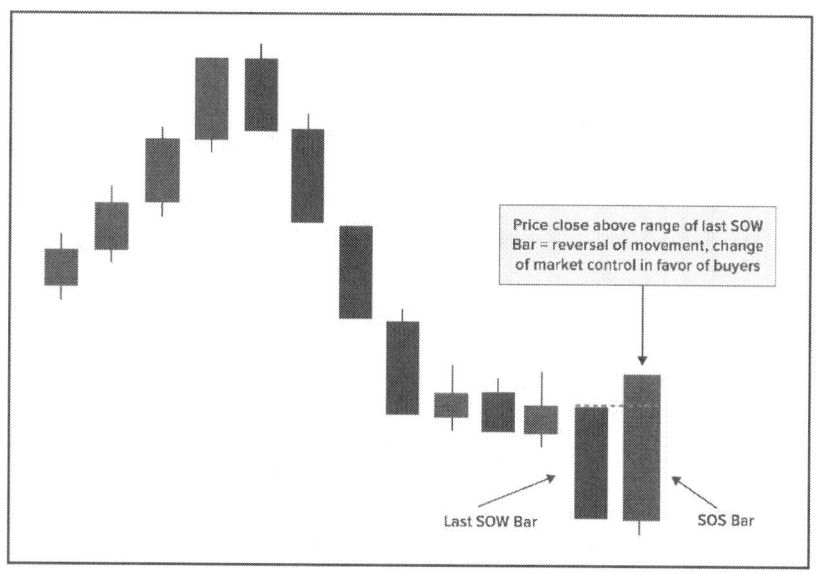

Example of change of market control from bearish to bullish

Position Management

We will now look at how to get in and out of the market. I strongly recommend sending all 3 position orders (entry, stop loss and take profit) at the same time to avoid potential electronic and emotional problems later.

It may be that in case of executing only the entry order and the price goes against us, we do not have the emotional capacity to place the stop loss where it would be initially. We could tremble at the point or even convince ourselves that that first location was too close and that the right thing to do would be to move it further away. We would simply be looking for a justification for not facing the reality of assuming a loss. The end result in most cases will be a higher than expected loss.

We could also suffer in that period of time some kind of electronic problem like an unexpected disconnection from the broker. That must be a very uncomfortable situation since you would find yourself with an open position and without any protection for it.

To avoid this kind of contingency, there is no reason not to launch the 3 orders directly. If the analysis is accurate, both the entry, stop loss and take profit will be perfectly identified before entering the market.

Calculate the size of the position

A very useful way to carry out proper risk management is to calculate the size of the position based on the distance between the entry level and the stop loss level.

In particular, I work with fixed position risk based on account size. This means that for each position a percentage of the total size deposited with the broker will be risked. It is recommended that this percentage does not exceed 1%.

To understand this well, the distance between the entry level and the stop loss level will determine the percentage of risk in the operation (for example, 1%). From there, the distance at which we locate the take profit will determine the ratio R:R (Risk:Reward) that will offer us that operation.

- A 1% of a 5000$ account is 50$. If our trade offers us a ratio of 1:3, with this type of management the possible monetary results would be: gain 150$ or lose 50$.

Depending on the type of trade, it is generally not recommended to take trades that have a negative R:R ratio; that is, the risk is greater than the reward.

The issue of position management is very broad and complex. I only wanted to leave this small point because it will be enough to carry out a more solid operation. I recommend looking for other readings where this section is more in-depth, as it is very worthwhile.

Entry

I return to the concepts previously studied because they will be very important for our trading: If we are after the downward breakage of the structure and the price is developing the upward movement that will develop the test after the breakage (potential LPSY), the appearance of a significant downward wing on the appropriate area (Ice) that closes below the minimum of the last significant upward wing could provide us with a good trading opportunity.

This is exactly what we will be looking for as an entry trigger before placing orders. In the background, it is the appearance in the short term of a strong volume (interest) that causes the development of a large intentionality candle (significant bar, SOS/SOW bar). We are at the right time and place.

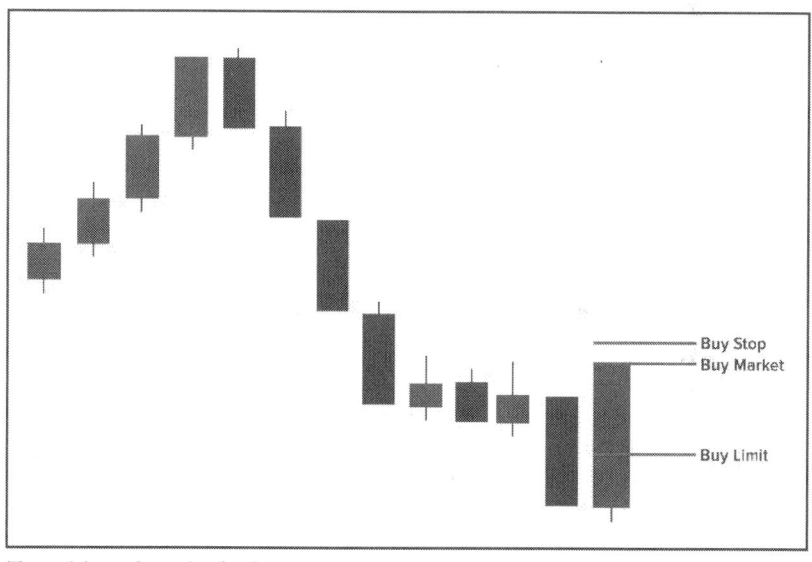

Types of buy orders to be placed

In view of the appearance of this expected event, we have no choice but to launch our orders to enter the market. Nowadays the platforms offer us different ways to do it:

- **Market orders**. It allows us to enter the market aggressively on the last cross price.
- **Stop orders**. It allows us to enter the market in a passive way in favor of the movement.
- **Limit orders**. Allows us to passively enter the market against the movement.

Types of sell orders to be placed

At this point I would like to emphasize again the importance of quantifying our entry trigger. As we see, there are many ways to enter the market, and each of them will have a different performance on the strategy. My recommendation is that you acquire the knowledge to perform a robust backtesting process in order to obtain the statistics that will provide us with objective results. This way we can compare the performance of the different ways we analyze to enter.

Stop Loss

The idea is to place the Stop Loss at the point where, if reached, the proposed scenario would be invalidated.

When placing the stop loss, we have to consider what type of entry we are facing. As a general rule, we will place the stop loss on the other side of the direction in which the significant bar (SOS/SOWbar) has developed, and on the other side of the whole scenario.

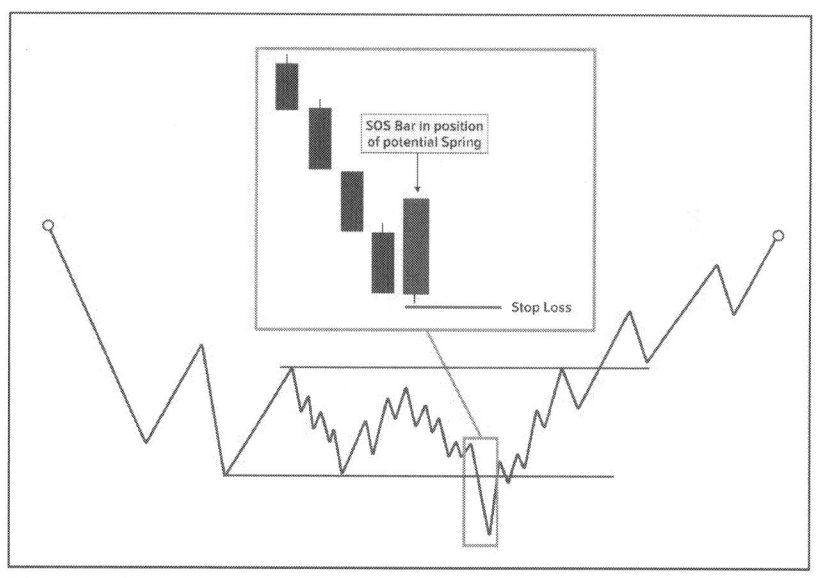

Placement of the Stop Loss in direct entry to the Spring

For entries directly into the shake, the stop loss should be located on the other side of the end:

- On a Spring, the stop should be below the minimum.
- On an Upthrust, the stop should be above the maximum.

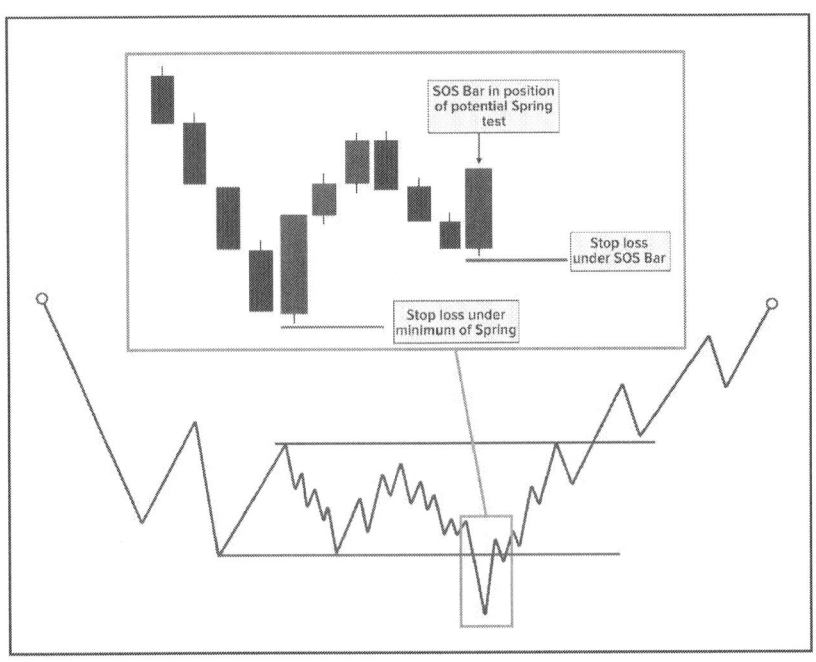

Placement of the Stop Loss at the entrance of the Spring test

    For entries in the shake test, we have two possible locations. One would be on the other side of the significant bar and the other would be at the end of the entire stage:

- In the Spring test, the stop would be either below the SOS-bar or below the minimum Spring.
- In the Upthrust test, the stop could be either above the SOWbar or above the maximum Upthrust.

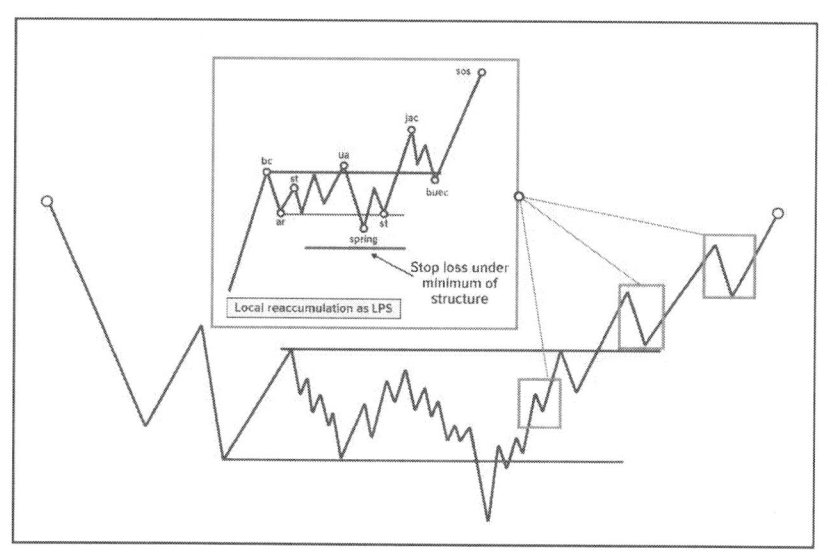

Placement of the Stop Loss at the entrance with a minor structure of reaccumulation

For inputs with a smaller structure it is best to place the stop loss at the end of the whole scenario:

- In minor reaccumulation structures, below the minimum of the structure.
- In minor redistribution structures, above the maximum of the structure.

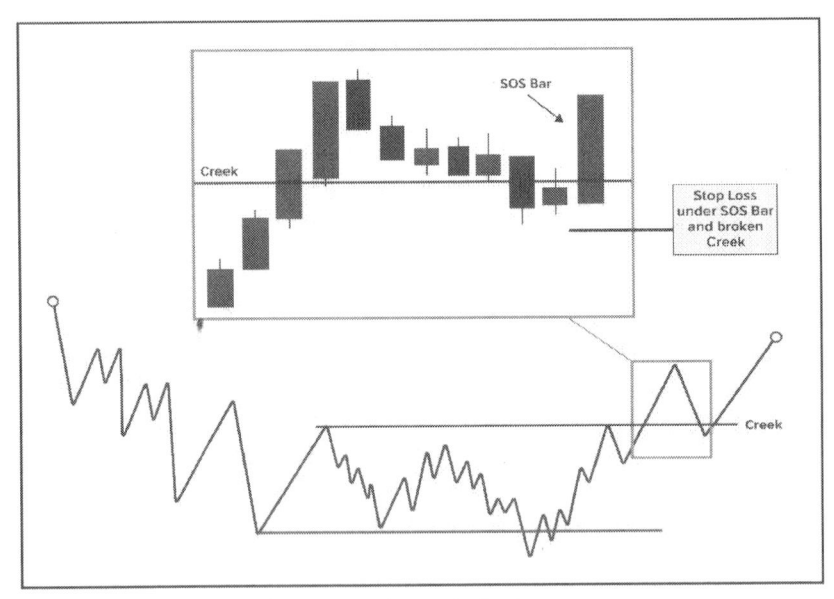

Placement of the Stop Loss at the entrance to the test after breakout

For entries to the break test, the stop loss would be far from the broken level and the significant bar in case we have used it as an entry trigger:

- In the breakout test (BUEC/LPS), the stop should be below the SOSbar and below the broken Creek.
- In the breakdown test (FTI/LPSY), the stop should be above the SOWbar and above the broken Ice.

Trailing Stop

Another way of managing the position is by using the trailing stop, which is based on changing the location of the stop loss as the price moves in our favour.

Although it may be a good idea, I particularly do not use them since due to their very nature, they do not leave much room for the price to move and as a consequence stop losses are easily reached.

In any case, it is a matter of testing and quantifying whether or not our strategy improves performance by incorporating this type of management.

Take Profit

Originally the Wyckoff methodology used point and figure charts to determine potential price targets.

We understand that the structure of the market today has changed too much to continue using that tool and therefore, operationally it seems much more useful to employ others.

Based on the pure analysis of the Wyckoff methodology, we will list the possible actions that we can use to take profit:

- **For evidence of climatic bar** (Buying Climax/Selling Climax) which will show high range, speed and volume. It would be an attempt to anticipate the stop of the previous trend, but it could be a sufficient signal to close the position or at least to reduce it.

It is a great way to exit the market when there is no price action to the left (at market extremes).

That lack of reference makes us go a little "blind" producing some operational inability. It is now more than ever that we must know how to listen to what the price and volume tell us.

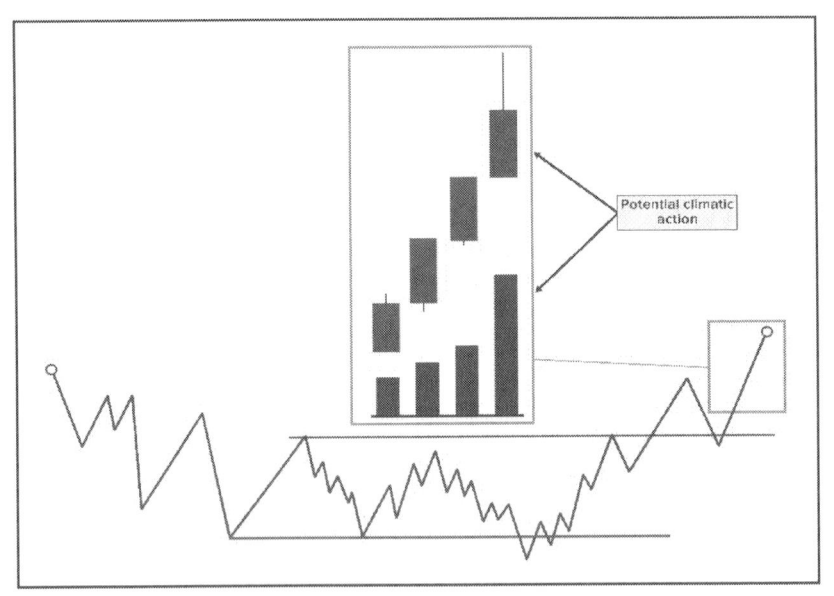

Profit taking on potential Buying Climax

A climatic volume at one end of the market is sufficient reason to abandon the position.

- **After the development of Phase A of stopping the previous trend.** The development of the first four events that delimit the appearance of Phase A will be sufficient reason to understand that the previous trend has ended and we must close our position.

Later the trend could resume in the same direction, but we cannot know this at that moment, so the most sensible thing would be to take profits.

It is important to note that the new structure should be developed within the time frame in which we have identified the previous structure.

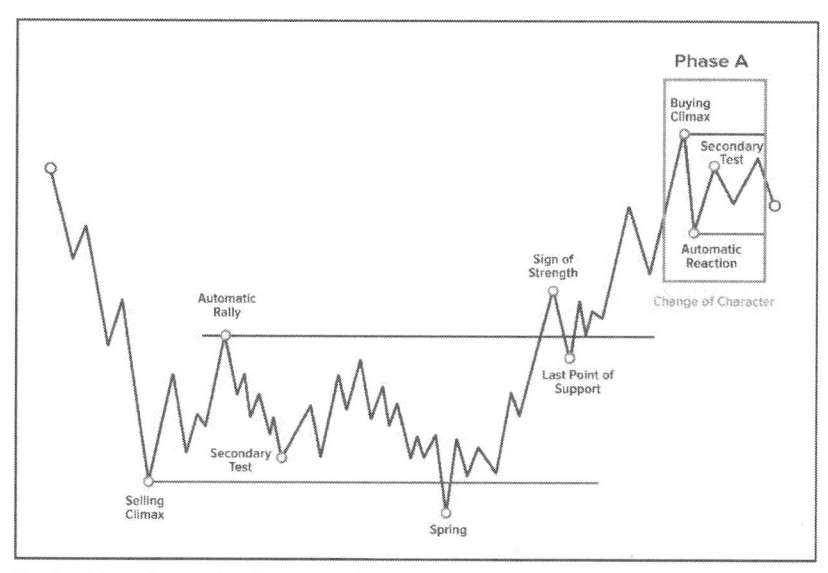

Profit taking after the development of a potential Phase A

Also, remember to put into practice the concepts of significant bar and motion reversal to more confidently identify the end of such events.

In addition to these possibilities, as we have previously discussed, we may want to use volume operating zones to locate our take profit orders. In this case, we will use:
- **Liquidity zones**. These are price turns; previous highs and lows. We know that in these zones there are always a lot of orders waiting to be executed and that is why they are very interesting zones to wait for the price to come in.

Some examples are the zones established by the structures: the minimums of the Selling Climax (in the acaccumulation structures) and the Automatic Reaction (in the distributive structures); and the maximums of the Buying Climax and the Automatic Rally.

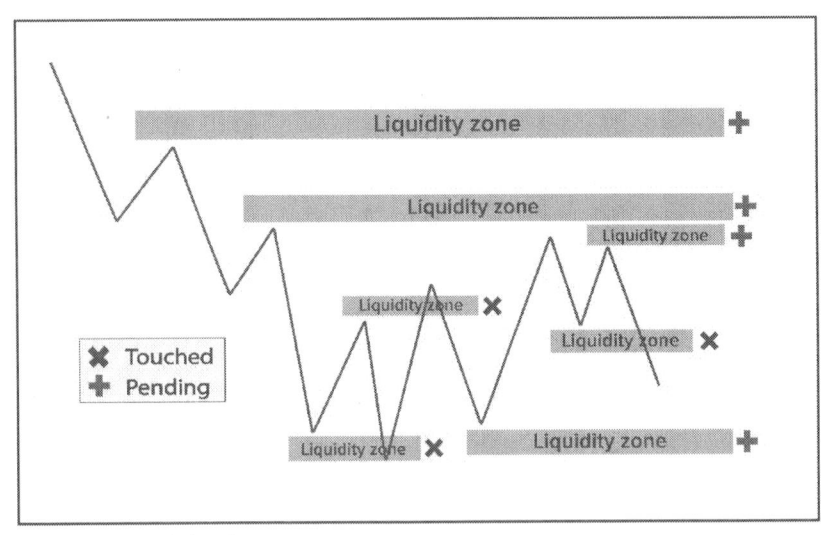

Establishment of the liquidity zones

Another example of liquidity zones to take into account as an objective of our operations are the previous liquidity zones (which are independent of the structures), both in our operational time frame and in higher ones.

The best way to take advantage of this reading is to identify the liquidity zones in the higher time frames and set them as targets. From there, use the structures developed by the price to enter the market with those price levels in mind.

We must consider that the market is constantly changing and will continue to generate new price turns (new areas of liquidity) so our objectives would have to be adapted to this new market information. That is, if we had originally established the profit taking in a distant liquidity zone, and in the development of the movement the price generates a new zone of liquidity closer, this should now also be considered.

- **Volume Profile levels**. The Volume Profile is a discipline based on a sophisticated tool that analyzes traded volume by price levels and identifies those that have generated the most and least interest. There are different types of profiles (session, range and composite) as well as different levels, the most prominent being

  - **VPOC**. Volume Point of Control. Determines the most traded level of the profile and therefore identifies the price with greater acceptance by both buyers and sellers. The logic behind this volume level is that, as it has previously been a level where both buyers and sellers have been comfortable crossing their contracts, it is very likely that in the future it will continue to have the same perception for all participants, causing a certain magnetism towards it.

Therefore, it will be advisable to have well identified the VPOCs of the previous sessions, the one of the current session, as well as the Naked VPOCs (old VPOCs that have not been tested again).

  - **VWAP**. Volume Weighted Average Price. Determines the volume-weighted average price at which a security was traded during the selected period. Being a reference level for institutional traders means that there is always a large amount of pending orders on it, and we already know that these orders act as a price magnet.

You can select the VWAP of the time period that best suits our operations. In general, the session VWAP will be more useful for intraday traders; the highest reference levels being the weekly and monthly VWAP.

Within the Volume Profile there are other levels that could be considered for the analysis, like the volume nodes (High and Low

Volume Node) and the value areas (Value Area High and Low); but the above mentioned are undoubtedly the most interesting ones for the operative. In any case, I recommend the in-depth study of this discipline since it is one of the best tools to enhance discretionary analysis.

It is also important to note that these volume operating areas are not only recommended to be considered for profit taking. As they are so relevant in the current operative, the most sensible thing is to have them identified at all times and to be able to take advantage of them also for entering the market and for the location of the stop loss.

A confluence of levels that would add solidity to the scenario would be, for example, to go short in a potential LPSY (after the bearish breakout of the structure) and that on the appropriate zone (context) our trigger candle (SOWbar) is developed whose range reaches in its superior part some level of volume (VPOC/VWAP) denoting a rejection to continue rising. You could enter at the end of the development of that significant downward wing and place the stop loss above the SOWbar, above the broken Ice and above the rejected volume level. As a goal, we could look for some of the possibilities proposed above.

Part 8 - Case Studies

Once the theoretical aspect of the methodology has been addressed, we will move on to analyse some real examples.

The basic structures studied serve as a reference to know approximately what to expect from the price; but the market by its very nature needs to move with a certain freedom. This is another of the strengths of the methodology with respect to other approaches, and that is that it combines the rigidity that events and phases provide with the flexibility required by the continuous interaction between supply and demand.

The point to highlight is that, although in the real market we are going to see many structures that are practically the same as the theoretical examples, this interaction between buyers and sellers is going to make each structure unique. It is practically impossible for two identical structures to be developed since this would require that the same operators who developed both structures be in the market at the same time and that they act in the same way. Mission impossible.

In case there is still any doubt about it, to say that the Wyckoff methodology is not only about correctly identifying the occurrence of events. The study of the entire theoretical section is an indispensable condition for solidifying the bases with the objective of developing judicious analyses and scenario proposals; but the approach goes much further. In the real operation, we will find examples of structures and unusual movements that we will have to know how to interpret correctly; and it is that as you advance each time you will have a smaller necessity of for example labeling all and each one of the actions since its identification will be instantaneous.

If, for example, we see a graph like the following one, where it seems difficult to label the structure correctly, that is not what is relevant; what is relevant is, if we manage to open this graph at the point I am pointing out, to have enough capacity to interpret this fluctuation as an accumulation structure and to be able to look for the incorporation in length.

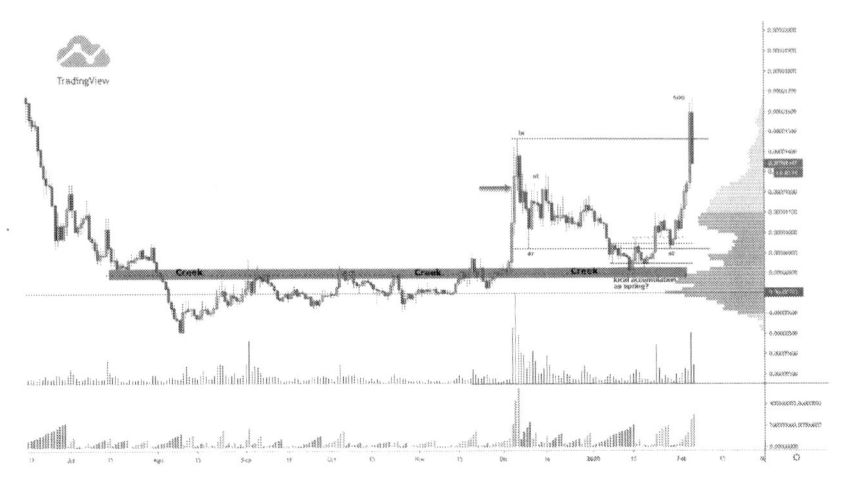

Example of unusual structure

That is where the real advantage of the Wyckoff methodology lies; it teaches us a way of reading the market from as objective a point of view as possible. Therefore, it is not a matter of identifying structures, events and phases to the millimeter as if we were robots.

Below we will see examples in different assets and time frames. It is important to note that when analyzing the assets we must do it on a centralized market so that the volume data is as genuine as possible. For the analyses, I have used the TradingView platform.

S&P500 Index ($ES)

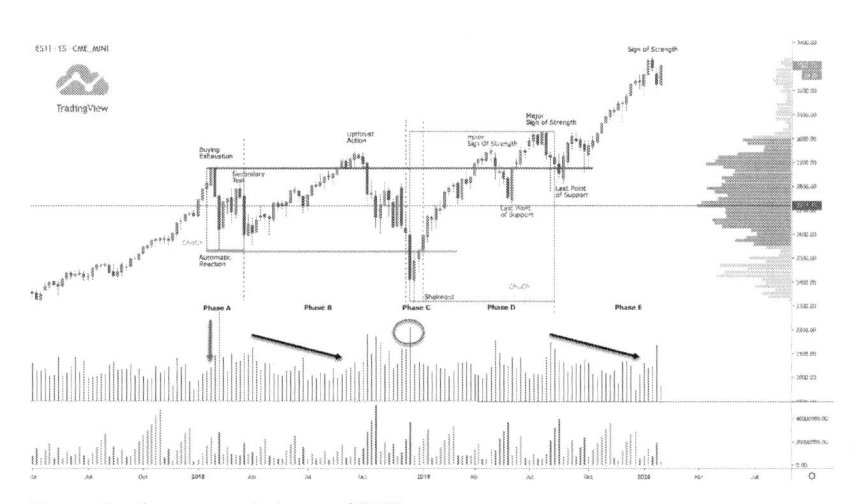

Example of reaccumulation on SP500

On the weekly chart, we see a classic reaccumulation structure with a shock.

This is a very good example to see the visual representation of what a Buying Exhaustion is. We see how the upward movement comes to an end without a volume peak that would identify the climatic event. With the Automatic Reaction and the Secondary Test the Phase A stop would be completed.

During Phase B we already see a certain background strength in developing this test at maximums (Upthrust Action).

Action that originates the test event in Phase C (Shakeout) with a relatively high volume. In this first part of Phase B we can see how the volume in general decreases, a sign that there is an absorption of stock by the buyers.

The upward reaction is unquestionable and leaves a new test at maximums that fails to produce the effective breakage of the structure (minor Sign of Strength). A small downward movement is necessary (Last Point of Support) before facing a new attempt to break upwards. On this second occasion, they manage to develop it (Major Sign of Strength) and the subsequent test (Last Point of Support) confirms that we are indeed facing a reaccumulation.

Very interesting how the price has initiated the trend movement out of the range in Phase E with a decrease in volume. This could suggest some kind of anomaly/divergence, but the supply/demand reasoning is clear: due to the absence of supply (there are few traders willing to sell), with very little demand buyers are able to push the price up.

Pound/Dollar cross ($6B)

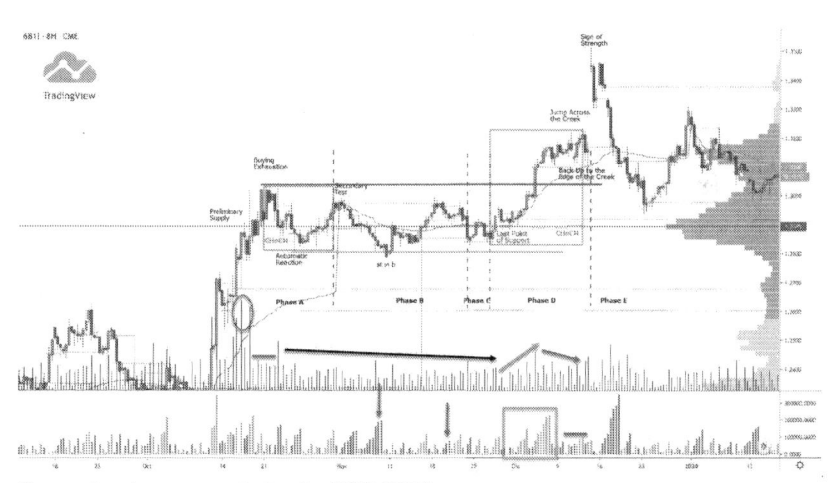

Example of reaccumulation in **GBP/USD**

Another bullish cross has formed on the 8-hour chart's Slow Stochastic, which means there is no sign of a major upward movement. As we mentioned before, these are difficult to trade as we will almost always be expecting at least some minor jolt from the inside of the structure.

We see another example of Buying Exhaustion after the appearance of a strong volume on the Preliminary Supply. This is one of the reasons why such exhaustion appears; and it is that if previously positions have been liquidated in an aggressive way, with little volume this turn will take place in maximums.

From the PSY's volume peak we see a decrease in volume until the beginning of the trend movement within the range after the Last Point of Support, suggesting absorption. Very visual also how the volume traded in the downward waves decreases denoting a loss of selling momentum.

Already in Phase D, we see an increase in volume and again very visually the rising Weis waves indicating this imbalance in favor of buyers. We have gone from a predominance of bearish waves to this appearance of bullish waves.

An important detail is the incorporation of the volume profile of the structure (horizontal volume that is anchored to the right of the chart) and how the VPOC of the structure (the most traded volume level) serves as a support to give rise to the LPS.

After the Jump Across the Creek event, the price develops a minor reaccumulation scheme based on confirmation (Back Up to the Edge of the Creek) with a clear decrease in volume, suggesting a lack of interest from sellers.

In this chart, we observe another very interesting element and it is that those big operators that were buying during the development of this structure took advantage of a fundamental event (in this case the negotiations for the BREXIT) to develop an enormous bullish gap as an effect of all this cause. This is not a coincidence and you will be able to see it in more occasions.

Euro/Dollar cross ($6E)

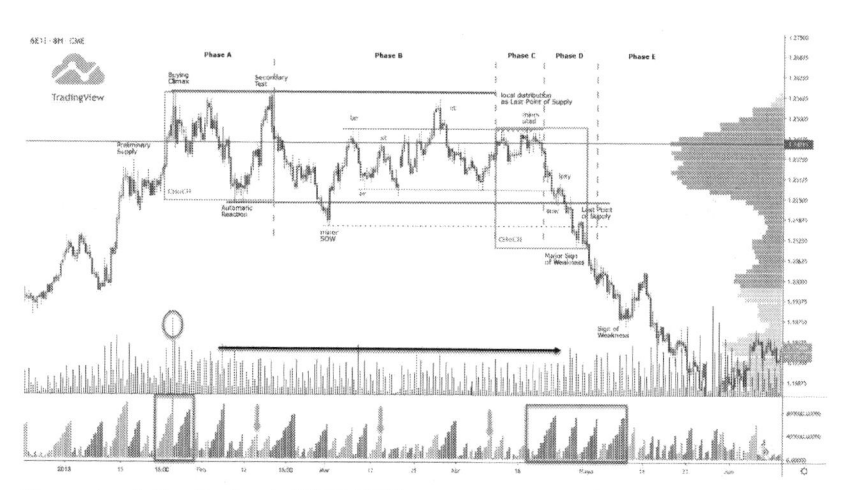

Example of distribution in EUR/USD

Basic distribution scheme without shaking. Here we see a clear example of the importance of context, in which the smaller structures fit into the larger ones.

After Phase A which stops the upward trend movement, the price starts Phase B during which a smaller structure develops inside it. The events of a distributive structure are clearly identified and how the minor UTAD (shake to relative highs within the range) gives rise to the downward trend movement of both the minor and the major structures.

We see how the VPOC of the structure's profile acts as resistance in the development of that UTAD minor, blocking further rises in the price.

After the Major Sign of Weakness, a brief upward reversal (Last Point of Supply) serves as a distribution confirmation test and gives rise to Phase E where the price quickly develops the downward movement out of range.

During the creation of the structure the overall volume remains relatively high, trace of the distribution ranges. In addition, Weis waves show the loss of momentum in the upward movement and an increase in the downward movement, being very noticeable in the last stages of the structure.

Bitcoin (BTCUSDT)

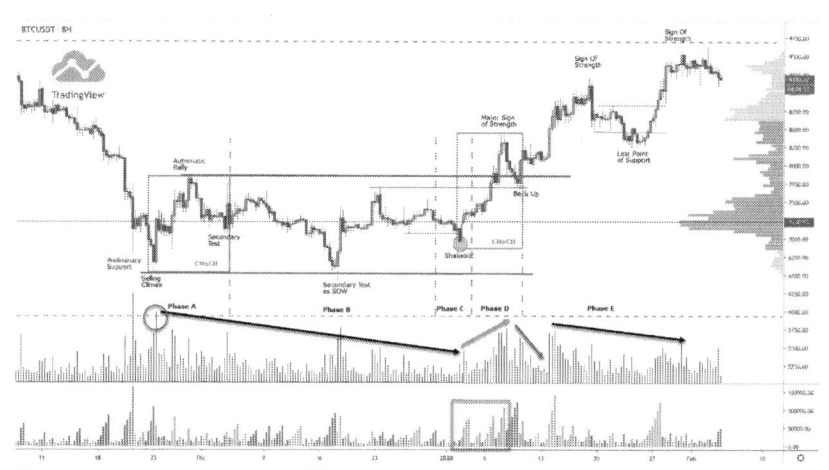

Example of accumulation in Bitcoin

As you know, reading under the Wyckoff methodology approach is universal and here we see a clear example of the Bitcoin graph.

Again we see a classic accumulation structure this time with a minor jolt as a test event in Phase C.

After the four stop events, during its development we see a decrease in the overall volume. First absorption signal and possible control of the buyers.

Although I have labelled the test at minimums in Phase B as a simple test in terms of sample weakness (ST as SOW), it could also have been seen as the Phase C Spring. The reasoning that has led me to do it this way is that the genuine Spring is automatically followed by the breaking movement, and as we see in this example, after that potential Spring the price is left lateralizing in the middle of the structure developing a minor scheme. But as I say, these are minor appreciations. The key will always be in determining where the final imbalance is occurring.

As I say, after that test in B, the price starts a minor structure right in the middle of the range, continuously interacting with the VPOC. It is in that minor structure that I consider Phase C to be occurring with that Shakeout that shakes off minor minima (minima within the structure). This is another good example of the importance of context. A minor structure of re-accumulation as a function of the Last Point of Support of the major one.

Here we can see how this shakeout does start the breaking movement almost immediately with that Major Sign of Strength. Later, the Back Up to the broken Creek confirms the accumulation structure with the appearance of a good SOSbar and starts the E Phase.

If we make a pure analysis of price and volume, we can see how it indicates harmony both in the breaking movement (price increase accompanied by volume increase) and in the retreat movement (price and volume decrease).

Already in Phase E we evaluate the trend and observe a certain loss of momentum evidenced by a new price momentum but with a lower volume. This does not mean that the price will turn around immediately; it is simply a footprint that suggests that there are fewer buyers willing to continue buying.

We could therefore expect some sort of more far-reaching reversal, but we have to bear in mind that the general context is that we have a bottom-up accumulation and that until the price develops a similar distribution structure we should continue to favour purchases.

Inditex (ITX)

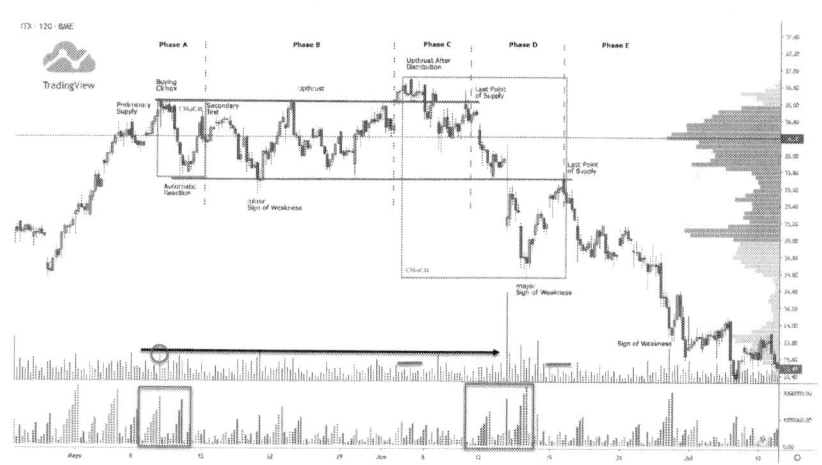

Example of distribution in Inditex

Inditex is a Spanish textile company. In this example, we see a classic distribution structure with a jolt on the 2-hour chart.

After the appearance of the climatic volume on the Buying Climax, the price develops an Automatic Reaction that is observed very visually by the Weis Wave indicator producing a very evident change of character (CHoCH).

Although it is true that there are certain moments of low activity in the general volume, certain peaks are observed throughout the development, mainly in the Minor Sign of Weakness and after the Upthrust After Distribution.

It is worth noting how the upward movement (UTAD) is carried out with a relatively low volume, pointing out the absence of interest to be quoted in those prices. The price produces an aggressive re-entry in the range that is stopped in the VPOC of the structure profile. A new bullish attempt is blocked by the sellers just in the high zone that establishes the maximum CB. This is the Last Point of Supply. A subsequent downward gap announces the aggressiveness of the sellers. The imbalance in favor of the bearishs has already materialized and the urgency to exit is evident.

In the Major Sign of Weakness movement the new change in character is observed but this time to announce the imbalance in favor of sellers. As always, very visual the Weis waves.

The subsequent upward movement with a decrease in volume would leave the last support point of the offer (LPSY) to start from there the trend movement out of the range in Phase E.

It seems to be a coincidence that this LPSY is produced in the lower part of the structure, in the broken Ice that establishes the minimum of Automatic Reaction; but it is not a coincidence, the markets generally have very identifiable operating zones and sometimes they leave us with very genuine structures as this example is.

Google (GOOGL)

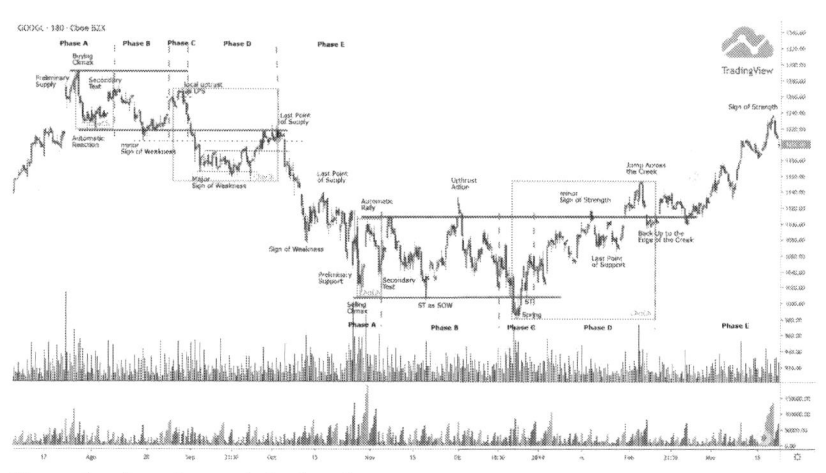

Example of market cycle in Google

With Google, we can study how the complete development of a price cycle with a distribution phase, downward trend, accumulation phase and upward trend is represented.

It is a graph that is already more complex to analyze but we can clearly see how the market moves; how it develops a distribution scheme as a cause of the subsequent downward trend; and how they need to make an accumulation campaign before starting the upward trend phase.

To be highlighted in the distributive structure is that test in Phase B that denotes weakness (minor Sign of Weakness), suggesting the possible imbalance in favor of the sellers, and how the Phase C event is a local shock at a relative maximum within the range. The reading is that buyers are so absent that they do not even have the capacity to drive the price to the top of the range. After the effective bearish break (Major Sign of Weakness) we can see the generation of a new minor redistributive scheme whose shock will test just the zone of the Ice of the major broken structure. Another new example of the importance of context, where the minor structures fit within the major ones.

In the lower part of the graph we analyze the accumulation scheme and again it seems to have been taken out of a book because the genuineness of its movements is fascinating. After the Spring in Phase C, the price fails to break the high part at first, leaving such a movement labeled as minor Sign of Strength. It requires a backward movement in which the price "takes a run" to jump the creek, recalling Evans' analogy with the Boy Scout. After the effective upward break (Jump Across the Creek), the price retreats to the zone and is refused to re-enter for up to two times before starting the out-of-range trend movement. This is a very good example of the importance of not re-entering the range. Buyers appear right in the critical zone to keep pushing the price.

Australian Dollar/US Dollar cross ($6A)

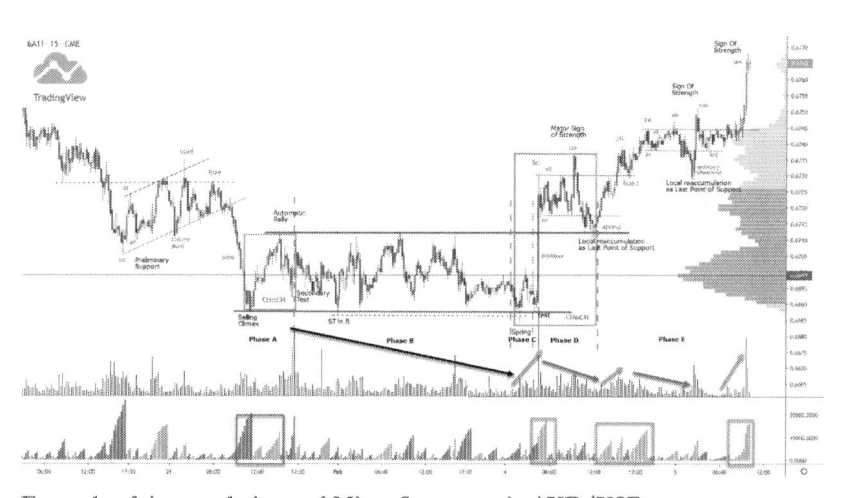

Example of Accumulation and Minor Structures in AUD/USD

In this last example, we are going to analyze a graph in temporality of 15 minutes. As already mentioned, this type of analysis does not know about time frames. It is a universal approach since it is based on the universal law of supply and demand. It is a perfect capture to exemplify what we understand by market fractality, where price develops the same structures although in different ways over all time frames.

On the left we see that the beginning of the accumulation campaign is born with a minor structure of redistribution in function of preliminary stop (Preliminary Support). In this case, this scheme is developed with a slight upward slope. Although they are not easy to see, this type of structure is also operable since, as we see, the events appear in the same way. The only thing to consider is that the slope of the structure will indicate if the market has greater strength or weakness in the background. In this example, we already see how that upward slope suggested a certain strength.

After the stop of the downward movement, we see a reduction of the volume during Phase B and a genuine Spring + test as Phase C. Classic development of the acaccumulation schematics.

Once the range is broken, the price manages to stay above it and creates a minor structure of reaccumulation with a shock that reaches the broken area, depending on the BUEC of the major structure. Very visual how the volume suggests a certain harmony at all times, being observed in increase on the impulsive movements and in decrease on the corrective ones.

Already during Phase E the market generates a new structure of reaccumulation with a new shakeout that serves to continue the price rise.

Making a correct reading in real time is complicated but we have to rely on all these signals to try to determine as objectively as possible who is in control. Context, structures and operational areas.

Thank you for buying this book!

Congratulations. With this book, you have taken the first step towards a successful career as a trader. I'd love to hear your opinion after you read it. I invite you to leave a rating in the Amazon reviews.

The content is dense and full of nuances. It is very difficult to acquire all the knowledge with a simple reading, so I recommend you to make a new study as well as personal notes for a better understanding.

But it doesn't end there. The book is too extensive but I left out many interesting things to tell you. I am currently writing a new book that I will send to the old buyers so I invite you to contact me at info@tradingwyckoff.com so that I can include you in the new list and you can receive the updates for free.

To give you an idea of the content to come, here I show you a draft of what will be the index:

Advanced concepts of the Wyckoff methodology
- The labels
- Price vs. Volume
  • Advanced chart types
- Accumulation or distribution failure

- Structural failure
    - Weakness
    - Strength
- Shortening of the Thrust (SOT)
- Other types of structures
    - Structures with a slope
        - Accumulation structure with an upward slope
        - Accumulation structure with downward slope
        - Distribution structure with an upward slope
        - Distribution structure with downward slope
    - Unusual schemes

Resolution of frequent doubts
- Efficient use of lines
- Changing labels and setting up scenarios
- How do you distinguish between accumulation and distribution?
    - Type of test in Phase A
    - Phase B test type
    - The shock in Phase C
    - Price and volume action in Phase D
    - The overall volume during the development of the range
    - The Weis Wave Indicator analysis
- How to analyze a graph from 0?
- Structures
- Operational zones
    - Temporary reduction
    - Temporary increase
- What to do when the context is not clear?

- Increasing the time frame
- Switching assets
    - The controller

The current trading ecosystem
- Types of participants in the financial markets
- Electronic markets
    - Algorithmic trading
    - High Frequency Trading
- Markets Over The Counter
- Dark Pools
- Are markets random or deterministic?
    - The adaptive markets hypothesis

The importance of volume
- Auction Market Theory
    - The variables
    - The perception of value
    - The four steps of market activity
- The Supply and Demand Law
    - Common errors of interpretation
    - BID/ASK, Spread and Liquidity
    - Types of participants based on their behavior
    - How the price shift occurs
- Initiative
- Lack of interest
    - How the market turns out
- Order types and crossing

- Tools for volume analysis
  - Order book
- Spoofing
- Iceberg Orders
  - Time & Sales
  - Footprint
  - Delta
- The Order Flow Problem
  - Problem #1. Price divergence
  - Problem #1. Divergence of delta
  - Price and volume operator
  - Conclusions
- Volume Profile
  - Auction Theory + Volume Profile
  - Composition of the Volume Profile
- Value Area
- Extremes
- Volume Point of Control
- Volume Weighted Average Price
- High Volume Nodes
- Low Volume Nodes
  - Types of profiles and uses
- Fixed range
- Session
- Composite
  - Difference between Volume Profile and Market Profile
  - Difference between vertical and horizontal volume
  - Uses of the Volume Profile

- Identification of structures
- Determining market bias
- Health trend analysis
- VPOC Migration
- P and b profiles.
- Calibration of position management
- Order Flow
    - Footprint reading
    - Imbalances
    - Rotation patterns
- Absorption
- Initiative
    - Continuation patterns
- Control
- Control test
    - Fractality

Wyckoff 2.0
1. Wyckoff Methodology
2. Auction Theory
3. Volume Profile
4. Order Flow
- Operation
    - Operational in trading ranges
        - In extremes
        - Inside
    - Trending operations
        - Interacting with the value zone

- Away from the value zone
- What do you do when the price goes up without us?
- Position management
    o Analysis
    o Entry
    o Stop Loss
    o Take Profit

Bibliography

Al Brooks. (2012). *Trading Price Action Trends.* Canada: John Wiley & Sons, Inc.

Al Brooks. (2012). *Trading Price Action Trading Ranges.* Canada: John Wiley & Sons, Inc.

Al Brooks. (2012). *Trading Price Action Reversals.* Canada: John Wiley & Sons, Inc.

Anna Coulling. (2013). *A Complete Guide to Volume Price Analysis:* Marinablu International Ltd.

Bruce Fraser. *Wyckoff Power Charting.* www.stockcharts.com

David H. Weis. (2013). *Trades about to happen.* Canada: John Wiley & Sons, Inc.

Enrique Díaz Valdecantos. (2016). *El método Wyckoff.* Barcelona: Profit Editorial.

Gavin Holmes. (2011). *Trading in the Shadow of the Smart Money.*

Hank Pruden. (2007). *The Three Skills of Top Trading.* Canada: John Wiley & Sons, Inc.

Hank Pruden. (2000). *Trading the Wyckoff way: Buying springs and selling upthrusts.* Active Trader. Páginas 40 a 44.

Hank Pruden. (2011). *The Wyckoff Method Applied in 2009: A Case Study of the US Stock Market.* IFTA Journal. Páginas 29 a 34.

Hank Pruden y Max von Lichtenstein. (2006). *Wyckoff Schematics: Visual templates for market timing decisions.* STA Market Technician. Páginas 6 a 11.

Jack. Hutson. (1991). *Charting the Stock Market: The Wyckoff Method.* United States of America: Technical Analysis, Inc.

James E. O´Brien. (2016). *Wyckoff Strategies & Techniques.* United States of America: The Jamison Group, Inc.

Jim Forte. (1994). *Anatomy of a Trading Range.* MTA Journal / Summer-Fall. Páginas 47 a 58.

Lance Beggs. *Your Traing Coach.* Price Action Trader.

Readtheticker.com

Rubén Villahermosa. (2018). *Wyckoff Basics: Profundizando en los Springs.* The Ticker, 1. Páginas 14 a 16.

Tom Williams. (2005). *Master the Markets.* United States of America: TradeGuider Systems.

Wyckoff Analytics. (2016) *Advanced Wyckoff Trading Course: Wyckoff Associates, LLC.* www.wyckoffanalytics.com

Wyckoff Stock Market Institute. (1968). *The Richard D. Wyckoff Course in Stock Market Science and Technique.* United States of America

Printed in Great Britain
by Amazon